MARY SHELLEY

GRAVE ROBBERS

Who shall conceive the horrors
of my secret toil, as I dabbled among
the unhallowed damps of the grave . . .

—FROM *Frankenstein*

THE STRANGE TRUE TALE
OF
FRANKENSTEIN'S
CREATOR
MARY
SHELLEY

CATHERINE REEF

CLARION BOOKS
Houghton Mifflin Harcourt
BOSTON NEW YORK

CLARION BOOKS

3 Park Avenue, New York, New York 10016

Clarion Books is an imprint of
Houghton Mifflin Harcourt Publishing Company.

HMHCO.COM

The text was set in Adobe Caslon Pro.
Title hand-lettering by Jamie Clarke.
Book design by Sharismar Rodriguez

Library of Congress Cataloging-in-Publication Data
Names: Reef, Catherine, author.
Title: Mary Shelley : the strange, true tale of Frankenstein's creator
/ Catherine Reef.
Description: New York : Clarion Books, [2018]
Identifiers: LCCN2018006981 | ISBN 9781328740052 (hardback)
Subjects: LCSH: Shelley, Mary Wollstonecraft, 1797-1851—Juvenile literature.
Authors, English—19th century—Biography—Juvenile literature.
Classification: LCC PR5398 .R44 2018 | DDC 823/.7 [B]—dc23
LC record available at https://lccn.loc.gov/2018006981

ISBN 978-1-328-74005-2

Manufactured in Malaysia
TWP 10 9 8 7 6 5 4 3 2 1
4500715382

For Kathy Henderson

So now my summer-task is ended, Mary,
And I return to thee, my heart's own home;
As to his Queen some victor Knight of Faëry,
Earning bright spoils for her enchanted dome;
Nor thou disdain, that ere my fame become
A star among the stars of mortal night,
If it indeed may cleave its natal gloom,
Its doubtful promise thus I would unite
With thy belovèd name, thou Child of love and light.

~Percy Bysshe Shelley

How like a star you rose upon my life,
Shedding fair radiance o'er my darkened hour!
At your uprise swift fled the turbid strife
Of grief and fear,—so mighty was your power!
And I must weep that now you disappear,
Casting eclipse upon my cheerless night—
My heaven deserting for another sphere,
Shedding elsewhere your aye-regretted light.
. . . .
And thought of you may linger in my dreams,
And Memory pour balm upon my pain.

~Mary Wollstonecraft Shelley

Contents

Artist Richard Rothwell painted this portrait of
Mary Shelley around 1840.

Prologue

*If the world is a stage and I merely an actor on it
my part has been strange, and, alas! tragical.*

Mary Shelley had been dead a year when her son unlocked her portable desk and found the remains of a human heart. The heart, he knew, had been his father's. It had rested in the desk for thirty years, unseen and untouched, since the day in 1822 when Mary Shelley tenderly wrapped it in pages of poetry and put it away. Dust and bits of dried-up muscle were all that was left.

The heart was a relic of past love. Like a powerful storm, this love had rolled through Mary Shelley's life, forever altering its course. For love of the poet Percy Bysshe Shelley, she turned her back on her family and gave up her place in the world. She sought bliss, and she found it, but she also found heartbreak that no one could have foreseen: suicides, drownings, and children born and lost. If a writer were to pack all this misfortune into one novel, readers would close the cover and complain that the book was too far-fetched.

But real life is more incredible than anything a novelist can invent, even one like Mary Wollstonecraft Shelley. In 1816, when she was eighteen years old, Shelley wrote *Frankenstein*. Her tale of dead flesh brought to life still frightens and fascinates readers today, two hundred years after it first appeared in print. Victor Frankenstein and the monster he built remain two of the best-known characters in literature and film.

Stories, even hideous ones like *Frankenstein,* are never created from nothingness, Mary Shelley believed. The storyteller draws on memory, on chance occurrences, on things read and overheard. From this chaos, she weaves a tale. "Every thing must have a beginning," Shelley wrote, "and that beginning must be linked to something that went before."

"I did not make myself the heroine of my tales," she stated about her writing. "I could not figure to myself that romantic woes or wonderful events would ever be my lot."

This book tells the true story of Mary Shelley—from its beginning, and with something of what went before. Was she the hero of her life's tale? That is for you, the reader, to decide.

CHAPTER ONE

Imagination

The solitary thoughts of the young are glorious dreams.

Dead hearts and bones can never be given new life. Still, Mary Godwin felt close to her mother in the St. Pancras churchyard. She often played alone among its neglected graves. A small child with a cloud of fine red-gold hair, she traced the letters on her mother's tombstone with her finger. The first name was the same as her own: M-A-R-Y. The next name was a long one, Wollstonecraft. Four-year-old Mary had no memory of her mother, who had died on September 10, 1797, eleven days after Mary was born.

From the portrait hanging in her father's study, Mary knew her mother as a fair-skinned woman in white. She looked fearless, like the heroine of romantic adventures, which some might say she was. She had gone to Paris during the French Revolution, which began in 1789, to support freedom and equality. In France she began a love affair with a rich American investor, Gilbert Imlay.

Her first daughter, Fanny Imlay, was born in 1794. Wollstonecraft followed Gilbert Imlay to England. Posing as his wife, she journeyed to Scandinavia to look after his business interests there. Then Imlay deserted her, and in despair, Wollstonecraft filled her pockets with stones and jumped from a wooden bridge into England's river Thames. She hoped to drown, but she was saved.

Wollstonecraft had also been one of the most forceful writers of her time. Her best-known book, *A Vindication of the Rights of Woman,* was published in 1792. An early feminist, Wollstonecraft

Mary Godwin stared often at this portrait of her mother, Mary Wollstonecraft, which hung in her father's study.

cried out in this book against a society that limited women's education, kept them dependent on men, and granted them few rights. The women held in highest esteem—the wives and daughters of the upper classes—were "the most oppressed," Wollstonecraft wrote. "How much more respectable is the woman who earns her own bread by fulfilling any duty, than the most accomplished beauty!"

Hardly anyone visited decaying old St. Pancras Church. The only voice Mary Godwin heard there belonged to the river Fleet, which flowed beyond the graveyard fence. The river did a dirty job, carrying filth and dead animals away from unfashionable Somers Town, on the northern edge of London. The Fleet poured its dark offerings into the Thames, whose water was said to make the best malt liquor.

A sandy path led Mary past smoking brickworks and fields of hay toward home. She trotted by workmen's cottages, watchmakers' shops, and the limping muffin seller making his rounds. As she neared

As a child, Mary Godwin found comfort at her mother's gravesite in the St. Pancras churchyard.

The dirty river Fleet flowed through shabby Somers Town.

the sixteen-sided housing cluster known as the Polygon, she heard snatches of French. Many of her neighbors had fled the revolution in France. They had come to England with little money and few connections, looking to start life anew. Mary lived at Number 29, the Polygon, with her father, William Godwin, and her half sister, Fanny.

Mary resembled her father, who was a small man with a high forehead and a long, narrow nose. William Godwin was devoted to words and ideas and had written novels, plays, biographies, and histories. In 1793, he had published a controversial book, *An Enquiry Concerning Political Justice*. In it, he attacked institutions that he believed stopped people from thinking in new ways or doing as they wished: marriage, schools, churches, and especially governments. "Whenever government assumes to deliver us from the trouble of

Dust heaps, such as this one in Somers Town, were a common sight in nineteenth-century England. Poor people sift through the piles of trash to find bits of discarded food, rags, lost jewelry, and anything else that might be sold.

The Godwins lived in the Polygon, the many-sided structure to the left, bordered by the curved sidewalk.

thinking for ourselves, the only consequences it produces are those of torpor and imbecility," he wrote. He imagined an ideal form of anarchy, one that did away with crime and let people share wealth equally. He was also an atheist.

Godwin was a longtime bachelor in January 1796, when he encountered Wollstonecraft at the home of a friend. He was leery at first, having heard that the feminist writer had a quick tongue. But she looked so sad that his heart went out to her. "Be happy. Resolve to be happy," Godwin coaxed. They began a friendship that grew into love. When Wollstonecraft became pregnant, she prepared to raise the child on her own, but Godwin would hear of no such thing. The man who had spoken out against marriage and religion joined with Mary Wollstonecraft in holy wedlock at St. Pancras Church on March 29, 1797.

When Wollstonecraft died, William Godwin grieved, but he held himself together. He had two little girls to raise and had to think about what to do. "I am the most unfit person for this office," he confessed. Nevertheless, he feared that the girls' Wollstonecraft aunts—his late wife's two unmarried sisters—might try to take one or both of them away. He had no legal claim to Fanny Imlay, after all. So he did his very best. He hired a wet nurse to feed the baby and a sunny nursemaid called Cooper to provide the children with daily care. He welcomed friends to come in and help. Among them was Maria Reveley, whose two children were playmates of Fanny's. She had studied painting in Rome and had married an architect, Willey Reveley, but they now lived apart. Godwin's sister, Hannah, who was a London dressmaker, also popped in regularly. His mother never left the farm where she lived, but she knitted socks and mittens for the girls and sent cloth for their frocks. In anxious letters she asked what baby Mary was eating and whether she was getting

Mary Godwin's father, author William Godwin.

enough fresh air. Godwin decided, however, that what he really needed was another wife.

One day in 1801, a woman approached him and asked, "Is it possible that I behold the immortal Godwin?" (Or so the family story went.) She was a new neighbor, "Mrs." Mary Jane Clairmont. She had two children, but whether there had ever been a Mr. Clairmont was an open question. Mary Jane Clairmont spoke French and had read many books, including William Godwin's. She kept a tidy house and had an affectionate nature. William Godwin liked her, and in December 1801, he married her.

His male friends saw the new Mrs. Godwin differently. To them, she lacked refinement and fell into foul moods. In other words, Mary Jane Godwin could never replace Mary Wollstonecraft, whom the friends remembered fondly. The men were in the habit of gathering in the Godwin home. They filled its rooms with rousing talk of science and world affairs. England was at war with Napoleon's France—which nation would prevail? Explorers were searching the Arctic—would they find a passage from Britain to India? An Italian scientist experimenting with electricity had made a dead frog's legs twitch—what else might be possible in the new century? Stimulating conversation formed the background noise of Mary Godwin's childhood.

Her father's friends were quirky but learned. Pale, high-strung Charles Lamb wrote essays on all kinds of topics, from gallantry in his own "modern" day to the glories of roast pig. Kindly James Marshall worked as Godwin's secretary and was willing to mind the children in a pinch. Marshall and William Godwin had once been students together. The statesman John Philpot Curran had thick brown hair that fell onto his forehead. He was a "great genius," Godwin said, with a "rich and inexhaustible imagination." Curran loved to plan trips overseas, but he grew homesick as soon as he left England. His unmarried daughter, Amelia, often sat beside him at Godwin's table.

Keen-witted Samuel Taylor Coleridge, who had strange red lips, could recite verses for hours on end. One night, Mary and her new stepsister, Jane Clairmont, sneaked out of bed and squeezed under a sofa to listen while Coleridge read his long poem *The Rime of the Ancient Mariner*. Mary thrilled to this eerie saga of an old sailing man. She shivered once as the mariner's ship sailed into a frigid region where "ice, mast high, came floating by." She quivered again as it sat in becalmed, stagnant waters, and "slimy things did crawl with legs / Upon the slimy sea." The girls' secret story time ended when Mary Jane Godwin yanked them from their hiding place.

Jane Clairmont was nearly Mary's age. She had dark eyes, springy black curls, and a smile for the world. Jane's brother, Charles, three years older, was an observant child. He had noticed that quiet Fanny often seemed unhappy. In 1803, Mary

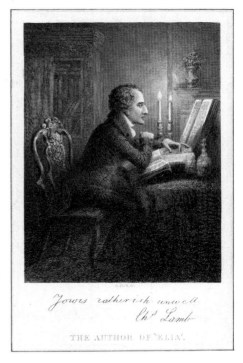

Jane Godwin gave birth to another boy, named William. He was a half brother to Mary, Charles, and Jane.

Charles Lamb was among the writers who gathered in the Godwin home for conversation.

One of the five children was quick to talk back and determined to have her own way. Mary was "singularly bold" and "somewhat imperious," Mr. Godwin declared. Mary disagreed. Her father was too strict and scolded her sharply for every small mistake, she thought. He was "too grave and severe." Perhaps Mary was right. If a father had "other objects and avocations to fill up the greater part of his time," as William Godwin said that he did, it seemed only natural for him to bark loudly at childish outbursts that might make another man smile.

William Godwin had to admit, though, that Mary was a good

student. The harder the lesson, the more she liked it. Charles Clairmont went to school, but the girls received instruction from William Godwin himself. Masters came to the home to teach them Italian and French, and Jane, who showed musical talent, had piano and singing lessons. William Godwin took the children on outings. They went with him to Westminster Abbey, the great London church where the nation's monarchs were crowned. He brought them to artists' studios and to the top floor of a commercial building, the Exeter Exchange, where lions, tigers, and monkeys were kept in cages. "Seeds of intellect and knowledge, seeds of moral judgment and conduct, I have sown," a self-satisfied William Godwin said.

Godwin believed the children should read—as long as they had books that made them think and imagine. He had seen too many children's books that drilled dry facts and proverbs into young heads. With those books, "we may learn by rote a catalogue of rules, and repeat our lesson with the exactness of a parrot," he pointed out, but we fail to dream. "Without imagination we may have a certain cold and arid circle of principles, but we cannot have sentiments."

At the start of the nineteenth century, Godwin could feel encouraged. New industries were creating a middle class with money to spend on its children. Some authors were creating books that engaged children's hearts and minds. They were writing poems about animals and fantasy stories with titles like *The Mermaid at Home*. Godwin began publishing his own books for young readers. He retold myths and fables. He put Bible stories into simpler language, wanting children to read them as historical tales from long ago. He also wrote biographies and histories of England, Greece, and Rome, all planned with children in mind. The young people in his own home were his first enthusiastic readers.

One day in 1805, Mary Jane Godwin suggested to her husband that they open a shop and sell children's books. To William Godwin, this sounded like a good idea. Children's books were becoming popular, and a shop would generate income. Somehow the household at Number 29, the Polygon, was always short of money. The couple started out small, with a kiosk at a busy street corner, selling books and stationery.

In 1807, William Godwin took out a loan and moved his brood into a bigger, costlier house, at 41 Skinner Street. The bookshop, to be called M. J. Godwin and Company, would occupy the first floor, and the family would live above it. An upper-story chamber would serve as a schoolroom. Ten-year-old Mary was sure her parents had made a huge mistake. The house seemed dingy and shakily built. And the location, in London's Holborn district, was far from prime. On Mondays, crowds gathered to watch as prisoners were paraded through the streets in open carts, on their way to the gallows. And Mary continually heard the cries of helpless animals being led to their deaths at the slaughterhouse nearby.

Godwin also rented a building next door to the Skinner Street home. There he housed his new publishing company, the Juvenile Library. He printed children's books authored by himself and his friends. The essayist Charles Lamb wrote several books for the Juvenile Library, including a children's version of the ancient Greek tale *The Odyssey*. Lamb insisted on leaving in the gory parts of the story. When a giant cyclops kills two sailors by "[dashing] their brains out against the earth," for example, Lamb describes how the monster "tore in pieces their limbs, and devoured them, yet warm and trembling, making a lion's meal of them, lapping the blood." These children's books were anything but dull.

This illustration of an enchanted cat is from a children's book published by Godwin's Juvenile Library.

Visitors to the house on Skinner Street saw a busy, noisy family. One person who came often was Aaron Burr. The former U.S. vice president was infamous for killing Alexander Hamilton, the first U.S. secretary of the treasury, in a duel. Burr had fled the United States in financial distress; while overseas he was hoping to refill his bank account and repair his reputation. Burr found Mary Jane Godwin to be "a sensible, amiable woman." The youngsters, he remarked, were "very fine children." Missing his own daughter, who was far away in South Carolina, Burr was charmed by the girls in the Godwin household, whom he called "les goddesses." Burr played games with the children, and he watched them put on shows. One evening, he listened as Jane sang a song and eight-year-old William gave a speech on "The Influence of Government on the Character of the People." It had been written by his stepsister Mary.

The home had its share of tears and scolding and talking back, yet it was as happy as any, even if the girls groaned when asked to help in the bookshop. But at thirteen, Mary was unwell. She was listless and wan, and eczema, an itchy red rash, covered one of her arms. It refused to go away no matter how many poultices the Godwins spread over it. In May 1811, hoping that sea air might help Mary's skin heal, they wrapped her arm in a sling and sent her to a girls' boarding school in Ramsgate, on England's southeast coast. A worried Mary Jane Godwin packed her off with a list of instructions: bathe often in seawater, see a doctor, and remember to apply your medicine. Money was tight: the family business was barely bringing in a profit, and loans had to be repaid. Nevertheless, if the change would help Mary, then it was worth the expense.

Mary's months at Miss Petman's Academy were lonely ones. School offered no nourishment for her hungry mind. In the first half of the nineteenth century, girls' schools instructed pupils in ladylike skills meant to help them fill idle hours, shine in society, and adorn their homes. They practiced dancing, drawing, speaking French, and doing fancy needlework.

Mary returned to Skinner Street after six months no healthier than when she left. When spring came and she still showed no improvement, her parents fixed their hope on a bracing northern climate. They arranged for Mary to stay with the family of William Baxter, an acquaintance connected to book publishing, who lived beside the River Tay, near the Scottish city of Dundee. Baxter was a widower with four daughters and two sons. "I do not desire that she should be treated with extraordinary attention, or that any one of your family should put themselves in the smallest degree out of their way on her account," William Godwin told him. Mary, he added, "will be perfectly satisfied with your woods and your mountains."

On June 7, 1812, Mr. Godwin, Fanny, and Jane escorted Mary to the dock where she boarded the *Osnaburgh,* the ship that would take her on the six-day voyage to Scotland. William Godwin approached another traveler, a woman whose three daughters were seeing her off, and asked if she would keep an eye on Mary during the voyage. The woman assured him that she would, but Mary rarely saw her once the ship left port. Mary was seasick for most of the trip, and somehow the money her parents gave her, which she had tucked into her corset, managed to disappear.

The family that welcomed her when she stepped ashore lived in a simple but cozy house overlooking the broad Tay. Ideas buzzed in the air in the Baxter home just as they did at 41 Skinner Street, because Baxter encouraged his children to read and think. Smart, brown-eyed Isabella Baxter, who quickly became Mary's friend, held Mary Wollstonecraft's writings close to her heart. She had studied so much about the French Revolution that she felt as if she knew the heroes and villains of that epic conflict. Mary and Isabella read aloud to each other from the folktales and traditional ghost stories of Dundee. Sometimes the Baxters took Mary on brisk hikes. They boated with her across the Tay to the town of Newburgh, where Isabella's oldest sister, Margaret, lived with her husband, David Booth. On one of those visits, the girls scratched their names into a pane of glass.

The hills and peaks surrounding Dundee had been stripped of trees by the city's busy shipbuilding industry. From Dundee, ships embarked to explore the unknown north or hunt whales. Whaling was dangerous work, especially in the frigid Arctic. Mary felt a horrific thrill upon hearing true tales of sailing men falling into bitter cold waters and drowning or being trapped on ice floes and freezing to death, or of ships that left Dundee and never returned.

While in Scotland, Mary Godwin watched boats sail in and out of the Dundee harbor.
Laden with supplies and sailing men, some headed for Arctic waters.

In Scotland, Mary felt uplifted, as if she had been dropped into an eagle's nest. She was in "the eyry of freedom, and the pleasant region where unheeded I could commune with the creatures of my fancy," she later recalled. Her surroundings inspired her to write. "It was beneath the trees of the grounds belonging to our house, or on the bleak sides of the woodless mountains near, that my true compositions, the airy flights of my imagination, were born and fostered," she stated. Though she would later lose those early stories, in Scotland this fledgling writer tried out her wings.

As an adult, she could summon back the intoxicating feelings of this time. "At fourteen and fifteen we only feel that we are emerging from childhood, and we rejoice," she wrote. Adolescence was "a dreamy delicious period, when all is unknown; and yet we feel that all is soon to be unveiled."

Whether from joy or healthy living, Mary's arm healed. Her smooth, clear complexion took on a healthy glow. When she smiled and shifted her light-brown eyes slyly to the side, young men were bewitched. Isabella's brother Robert fell quite in love with her.

Letters from home told Mary about new friends who had begun calling at Skinner Street. Percy and Harriet Shelley were a young married couple. The elder son in a wealthy family, Percy Shelley had begun writing poetry at an early age. Shelley was quick to act on his impulses and he could never sit still. He felt ready to change the world. While students at Oxford, he and his friend Thomas Jefferson Hogg wrote and published *The Necessity of Atheism,* a pamphlet insisting that God's existence could not be proved. It was a radical enough statement in 1811 to get the young men called into the master's office. Lying to the master about their authorship was a worse offense, and this is what got them expelled. Then, at nineteen, Shelley had eloped with Harriet Westbrook, one of his younger sisters' schoolmates.

When Shelley read William Godwin's book *An Enquiry Concerning Political Justice,* its call to reject stifling institutions seemed to be directed at him. He had assumed that William Godwin was an old author, long dead. Surprised to learn in 1812 that the revered writer was alive and living in London, Shelley wrote him a letter. Soon the Shelleys were frequent guests in the Godwin home. Percy Shelley gave William Godwin a copy of his long poem *Queen Mab,* a political message wrapped in a fantasy tale. In *Queen Mab,* Shelley takes his readers on a chariot ride across the heavens to view a future utopia. The past and the present, also on view, are marred by humanity's institutions, especially monarchy and religion. At the end of the poem, Shelley tacked on more than a hundred pages of notes in which he argued against the existence of God. No commercial

Harriet Westbrook was a sixteen-year-old schoolgirl in 1811, when she eloped with Percy Shelley.

publisher would touch such an inflammatory work, so the poet paid to have a small number of copies printed.

William Godwin was less impressed with Percy Shelley's poem than with his purse. One day the youth would possess the estate of his well-to-do father, Sir Timothy Shelley. Sir Timothy had stopped Percy's allowance upon his marriage to Harriet, of which he disapproved, but Percy had other ways of getting funds. He borrowed here and there, sometimes taking out "post-obit" loans. In other words, lenders advanced him sums based on his future inheritance. In exchange, Percy agreed to pay back that amount—plus a great deal of interest—when his father died. For a post-obit loan of two thousand pounds, for example, Shelley would have to pay the lender six thousand pounds after his father's death. William Godwin liked the fact that Shelley had access to money. He believed that wealth was meant to be shared, and why not with himself?

In November 1812, Mary went home to Skinner Street for a visit, accompanied by Isabella's sister Christy, William Baxter's oldest unmarried daughter. Whether Mary met the Shelleys at this time is unknown, but Christy Baxter did. Percy Shelley was tall, she noted, with large blue eyes and a penetrating gaze. He leaned forward when he walked, as though his mind moved faster than the rest of him, and his curly brown hair needed combing. Unlike most gentlemen, he seldom wore a hat when he went out, and he left the collar of his shirt unbuttoned. Harriet Shelley, in her purple satin dress, stood out from the plainly clothed women in the Godwin family.

After seven months in England, Mary returned with Christy to Scotland. She stayed until March 1814, and cried when she left again, never to return. Seventeen-year-old Robert Baxter followed her to London, hoping for a promise of marriage, but love would lead Mary to someone else. She was soon to imagine a different life.

CHAPTER TWO

Escape!

Love is to me as light to the star.

Percy Shelley's friends called him by his last name or by his middle name, Bysshe ("Bish"). On June 8, 1814, on a London street, he ran into his college chum Thomas Jefferson Hogg. Hogg, a student of law, had just come from court. He walked with Shelley, who was hurrying toward Skinner Street. "I must speak with Godwin," Shelley said when they reached number 41. "Come in, I will not detain you long."

They entered the bookshop and learned that Godwin was out. Hogg recalled, "Bysshe strode about the room, causing the crazy floor of the ill-built, unowned dwelling-house to shake and tremble under his impatient footsteps. He appeared to be displeased." Again and again Shelley asked, "Where is Godwin?" Each time, Hogg could only say that he did not know.

A door into the shop partly opened, and Hogg recorded what happened next: "A thrilling voice called 'Shelley!' A thrilling voice answered, 'Mary!' And he darted out of the room, like an arrow from the bow of the far-shooting king." Hogg glimpsed "a very young female, fair and fair-haired, pale indeed, and with a piercing look." She wore a bright Scottish-plaid dress that stood out from the colorless clothing commonly worn in London. Shelley was gone for a minute or two. When he returned, he had lost interest in seeing Godwin—if that had ever really been his goal.

As time went on, Hogg reflected on that day. Clearly, Percy Shelley and Mary Godwin had met before then. But, Hogg asked himself, "Do you think he loved her?" It seemed as though he did. "First impressions are indelible," Hogg remarked, "and in them alone are the truth and reality of things for the most part to be found." Percy Shelley became a daily caller at Skinner Street. Harriet Shelley and their year-old daughter, Ianthe, were miles away, staying in the spa city of Bath.

Shelley was bored with Harriet. He regretted his hasty marriage, and now he had found a girl with whom his wife could never compare. Harriet had been brought up to please others rather than think for herself. Mary Godwin, however, was the child of two great minds. She had read many books and could hold her own in conversation. Harriet, with her small features and neat brown hair, was a pretty doll. But Mary was a sight to behold! Jane Clairmont described Mary's hair as being "of a sunny and burnished brightness like the autumnal foliage when played upon by the rays of the setting sun." It was so fine that it looked weightless, "as if the wind had tangled it together into golden network."

In early June, Shelley wrote a poem to Mary and slipped it to her across the bookshop counter:

A young Percy Bysshe Shelley.

Upon my heart thy accents sweet
Of peace and pity fell like dew
On flowers half dead;—thy lips did meet
Mine tremblingly . . .

The poem reveals that the pair had kissed.

Mr. and Mrs. Godwin never suspected that anything improper might be going on. William Godwin had money on his mind. He was helping Shelley obtain another post-obit loan and expected to receive a share in thanks. Godwin told himself that if Shelley dined at Skinner Street every day, it was because he relished the literary talk. If Mary and Shelley took long walks—well, they had to be innocent, since Jane went too.

The walks took Mary, Shelley, and Jane to the St. Pancras churchyard, where they sat on Mary Wollstonecraft's grave and talked about life and the future. All three had grown up on Wollstonecraft's words: "Gain experience—ah! gain it—while experience is worth having, and acquire sufficient fortitude to pursue your own happiness." Through her books, she spoke directly to them. Eager for experience, they were all Wollstonecraft's children in spirit.

On Sunday evening, June 26, Jane perched on a tombstone at the far side of the cemetery while Mary and Shelley spoke alone. Mary never forgot how Shelley opened his heart to her, "at first with the confidence of friendship, & then with the ardour of love." Nor would Shelley forget his joy when Mary said that she returned his affection. "The sublime and rapturous moment when she confessed herself mine," he said to Jefferson Hogg, "cannot be painted to mortal imaginations." The pair walked back to Skinner Street arm in arm.

Soon afterward, Shelley told William Godwin that he and Mary were in love. If he thought Mary's father would take the news well, he was badly mistaken. Godwin's views on marriage had softened in the twenty-one years since he had published *An Enquiry Concerning Political Justice*. He had even married twice himself. Now Shelley, who had a wife and child, was romancing another woman, and that woman was his own beloved daughter, a mere girl of sixteen. Godwin was furious. "I could not believe that you would enter my house under the name of benefactor, to leave behind an endless poison to corrode my soul," he said. "I would as soon have credited that the stars would fall from Heav'n for my destruction."

Godwin made the younger man promise "to give up his licentious love, and return to virtue." He banished Mary to the upstairs schoolroom. Once the post-obit loan was finalized, on July 6, he ordered Shelley to stay away from Skinner Street. But irate fathers and promises made under pressure are no match for the sheer force of love—as William Godwin was about to find out.

Mary and Shelley had a trusted ally in Jane, who sneaked their letters in and out of Mary's schoolroom prison. Shelley, forbidden to see Mary, was frantic. "His eyes were bloodshot, his hair and dress disordered," observed the writer Thomas Love Peacock, a friend of Shelley's who had called on him in London. "Nothing that I ever read in tale or history could present a more striking image of a sudden, violent, irresistible, uncontrollable passion, than that under which I found him laboring." Shelley snatched up a vial of laudanum, a medicine made from opium that was toxic in high doses. "I never part from this," Peacock heard him say ominously.

Laudanum was a key ingredient in one woman's recipe for a cholera cure. In truth, this concoction was no more effective than any other treatment used at the time to combat infectious diseases.

Meanwhile, Harriet, hearing nothing from her husband for several days, went to her father's house in London. She met with Shelley, who informed her that he worshiped Mary, body and soul. He still cared for Harriet, but he explained to her, "Our connection was not one of passion & impulse. Friendship was its basis." This was no one's fault, not Harriet's and not his own. "It is no reproach to me that you have never filled my heart with an all sufficing passion," he added. Harriet, who was pregnant, tried to remain dignified, but she blamed Mary for seducing Shelley away from her.

A few days later, Shelley burst into the bookstore on Skinner Street. William Godwin was out; his friend and secretary, James Marshall, awaited his return. Shelley "looked extremely wild," Mary Jane Godwin said. Pushing past Mrs. Godwin, he rushed upstairs and into the schoolroom. He gave Mary the bottle of laudanum and told her to swallow its contents. "They wish to separate us, my beloved," he said, "but Death shall unite us." Then he pulled out a pistol. He was going to shoot himself so they could be together in death like Romeo and Juliet.

Mrs. Godwin and James Marshall stepped into a chaotic scene. Jane was shrieking; Mary, pale and crying, was begging Shelley to calm down and go home. "I won't take this laudanum," she said. "But if you will only be reasonable and calm, I will promise to be ever faithful to you." Marshall helped Shelley get control of himself, and the poet departed, leaving the laudanum on a table. A few days later he took an overdose of laudanum himself, but his landlady discovered him in time to summon a doctor, who saved his life.

The Godwins had good cause to oppose Mary's involvement with Percy Shelley. Not only did he have a wife and family, but he had shown himself to be unstable. Also, Mary needed to protect her reputation. For a young man to sow some wild oats was accepted and considered natural. Society judged him on his wealth and his work, if he had a profession. But the public's opinion of a girl rested on her innocence. By tarnishing her reputation—even through an unwise flirtation—she risked spoiling her chances of marrying well. Sharing intimacies with a married man was especially ruinous. Polite society would shun her. Genteel ladies would turn their backs to her, now and for years to come.

Mary understood these things, but her heart was in turmoil. She had fallen in love, deeply and unexpectedly, at a young age, and she struggled with new feelings and priorities. One future mattered to her, a life with Percy Bysshe Shelley. Shelley meant everything; she could be happy only with him. When she wrote years later that "love, though young and unacknowledged, will tyrannise from the first, and produce emotions never felt before," she drew on her youthful experience.

After Jane's role as messenger came to light, she, too, was confined to the house. Shelley then bribed a servant to carry his letters to Mary. In this clandestine way, he and the two girls hatched a plan.

They put it into action on Thursday, July 28. At five a.m., with the sun about to rise, Mary placed a letter on her father's dressing table, where he would see it when he woke up. She and Jane, wearing black silk traveling dresses, crept silently down the stairs and out of the house. The girls held bundles, and Mary carried a small box containing papers she treasured: stories she had written, letters from people dear to her, and old love notes that had been exchanged between Mary Wollstonecraft and William Godwin. The girls hurried along sleeping streets to a corner where Shelley waited with a carriage and driver. "She was in my arms—we were safe," Shelley said with relief. He and Mary were escaping to France and Switzerland to begin their life together. Foreign sights and experiences were going to open their minds—or so they hoped. "The art of travelling is only a branch of the art of thinking," Mary Wollstonecraft had written.

Why Jane went along is anyone's guess. She may have craved adventure or had her own reasons for escaping home. She had been the lovers' confidante since their romance began and may have hoped to continue in that role. She also believed her unknown father was Swiss and may have longed to see his homeland. Whatever her reason, Mary and Shelley welcomed her.

The adventurers rode swiftly in case they were being pursued, pausing only when Mary's motion sickness forced them to take a break. Every hour placed miles between their carriage and London. Twelve hours of travel brought them to the southern port of Dover, where they decided against waiting for the morning packet, the commercial vessel that carried mail and passengers across the English Channel. Instead they hired some sailors to take them to France overnight in a small open boat.

A gentle breeze blew as they embarked, but toward daybreak they sailed into a thunderstorm, and their boat rose and fell with the swelling sea. Leaning against Shelley's knees as waves washed over the sides of the craft, a seasick Mary felt him trembling. In time the squall passed, and Mary fell asleep. She woke hearing Shelley call softly, "Look, Mary, the sun rises over France." Wind had pushed the boat onto a beach near the northern French town of Calais.

That evening, the three were resting at a hotel when the innkeeper informed them that an English lady had arrived, seeking her daughter. Mary Jane Godwin had set out as soon as she and her husband read Mary's note, which told them the trio was bound for France. Mary's reputation was ruined, but Mrs. Godwin hoped she

Wind and rough waves could make crossing the English Channel
difficult and even dangerous.

had time to save Jane's. Having caught up with the runaways, she
ordered Jane to spend the night in her room. She planned to return
home the next morning with Jane, and all would be well, as far as
her own daughter was concerned.

All *was* well until daylight came and Shelley managed to speak
to Jane. Emboldened by his urging, Jane defied her mother. She
would stay right where she was, Jane declared. She was going to
journey on with Mary and Shelley. Too angry even to speak, Mary
Jane Godwin marched out of the hotel and sailed back to London
alone.

Journeying on meant venturing farther into France, where
everything from food to fashion was strange and novel to the three
young Britons. They poked at plates of fried artichoke leaves, thinking they might be frog meat. They stared at the people of northern
France in their traditional clothes. Mary commented in a journal

on "the women with high caps and short jackets; the men with ear-rings." In Paris, she and the others wandered past paintings in the Louvre. They saw the great cathedral of Notre-Dame and walked in the famed Tuileries Garden, which Mary found formal and dull. She was happiest lying beside Shelley in their cheap hotel. Wrapped in his embrace, she lived in the moment, without a worry for the future. Said Shelley, "Our own perceptions are the world to us."

Shelley had dashed off without the funds from his latest post-obit loan, so pretty soon the travelers were short of money. Shelley

The traditional dress of northern France included high white caps for women and full breeches for men. These costumes appeared exotic to the trio of English travelers, who had seen very little of the world.

sold his watch and managed to borrow sixty pounds, and they used some of the cash to buy a donkey. For four days they walked south and east across the countryside toward Switzerland while the donkey carried their bundles.

The long war with France had recently been won; Napoleon was exiled to Elba, an island in the Mediterranean Sea. Russian soldiers, retaliating for Napoleon's 1812 invasion of their country, had ravaged the French landscape. Mary, Shelley, and Jane saw burned-out cottages, churches, and shops, and hungry, impoverished people. Where once there had been a large village, "now the houses were roofless," Mary observed. "The ruins that lay scattered about, the gardens covered with the white dust of the torn cottages, the black burnt beams, and squalid looks of the inhabitants, presented in every direction the melancholy aspect of devastation." They walked many miles before they spotted crops growing. One day, milk and sour bread was the only dinner they could buy. The inns where they slept were filthy and teeming with rodents. One night, Jane squeezed into bed with Mary and Shelley after a rat walked across her face and sent her scurrying from her own room.

The donkey proved too frail for such a long trek, and pretty soon it refused to budge. The three runaways half carried it to a nearby village, where they sold it and bought a mule that they could ride. They took turns in the saddle until Shelley sprained his ankle and the girls insisted he do all the riding. After a week of this, Mary and Jane grew weary of trekking in the heat. The mule was sold and a small carriage purchased. Money also went to hire a driver.

Shelley was flying high. He dreamed of forming a community of free spirits in Switzerland and wrote to Harriet, inviting her to come. "You will at least find one firm & constant friend, to whom your interests will be always dear, by whom your feelings will never wilfully be injured," he assured her. He could not understand why Harriet found such a letter hurtful or why she never responded. When a beautiful little girl charmed Shelley in the town of Champlitte, he tried to talk her father into letting him adopt her. The father of course refused.

Days and weeks passed in slow, steady travel. On August 19, Jane spotted something far off that looked like bright, flaky clouds. "What was my surprize when after a long & steady examination I found them really to be the snowy Alps," she wrote. "Yes, they were really the Alps"—still a hundred miles distant. As they drew closer and made out the shapes of mountains, Shelley was overjoyed. "On every side their icy summits darted their white pinnacles into the clear blue sky," he wrote. He imagined he was looking at the crumbling remains of ancient temples: "Blue vapours assumed strange lineaments under the rocks and among the ruins, lingering like ghosts with slow and solemn step."

The beauty and grandeur of the Alps filled Mary, Percy, and Jane with awe.

By the time they reached Switzerland, everyone was cross. It rained all the time. Mary's stomach was upset. She realized that she had left her box of treasured papers at a hotel in France and would never see it again. Unable to find a cottage to rent, the three leased an ugly apartment. They were getting on one another's nerves, and they were running out of money. By August 27, they had twenty-eight pounds, barely enough to get home. Everyone was ready to go.

They returned by river because it was cheaper and faster than going overland. Mary turned seventeen in the northern Swiss city of Basel. She and Shelley read to each other from one of Mary Wollstonecraft's popular works, *Letters Written during a Short Residence in Sweden, Norway, and Denmark*. This slim volume was more than a travel book. Wollstonecraft had used her time in Scandinavia to explore her inner life. She delved into the power of nature to inspire the imagination. A soul in harmony with nature "sinks into melancholy, or rises to extasy," she wrote.

Picturesque Germany made all three travelers ecstatic. Small islands rested in placid blue waters in some sections of the winding Rhine River. White rapids crashed against rocks in other spots. Hills rose along both banks, their thick covering of trees broken here and there by villages and steeples. In early September, the barge moored briefly at Gernsheim, near the ruins of Frankenstein Castle, the birthplace, in 1673, of the alchemist Johann Konrad Dippel. Dippel was known for experimenting on dead animals and claimed he had discovered the elixir of life, a potion that made people immortal.

Blustery, wet weather greeted Mary and her companions when they reached the Dutch port of Rotterdam. They boarded a packet bound for England on Friday, September 9, with the understanding that they would pay their fare when they reached their destination. Soon, wind and heavy seas forced the captain to turn back

The ruins of medieval castles rose from rocky heights along the Rhine.

and seek safety in Maassluis, another Dutch town. Held up for two days by storms, Mary, Jane, and Shelley had almost nothing to eat. They wrote to pass the time. The titles of the girls' stories reflected their moods: Mary's was called "Hate," and Jane titled hers "The Ideot." Shelley worked on a longer, gothic tale that he was calling *The Assassins.*

At last, on Sunday, September 11, conditions had improved enough for the packet to set off again, although the North Sea was anything but calm. "The face of the Captain was all anxiety," Jane saw. She was the only person on board to escape seasickness. Mary felt queasier than most, but her illness was due to more than the pitching of the boat. She was pregnant.

CHAPTER THREE

Life's Lessons

*While we are young, we feel as if happiness were
the birthright of humanity; after a long and cruel
apprenticeship, we disengage ourselves from this illusion.*

When the packet reached England, Mary, Shelley, and Jane confessed that they had no money. The captain saw three young people who seemed too clever for their own good, and he was far from pleased. He sent a boatman with them to London, with orders to collect what the passengers owed. The boatman waited while Shelley went into his bank and was denied credit. He looked on as acquaintances turned down Shelley's pleas for a loan. Finally, he sat for a long time with Mary and Jane in a coach outside Harriet's father's house while Shelley talked his wife into giving him the cash he needed.

Their fare paid, Mary and her companions settled in dim, dirty rooms. They soon moved to an even cheaper place near the Polygon and St. Pancras Church. By choosing to be with Percy Shelley, Mary Godwin had embarked on a life of wandering and scraping by.

She also was learning how it felt to be an outcast. When she first came back to England, her father had been ready to welcome her home. In his mind, William Godwin saw Mary coming to him and confessing her mistake. He imagined himself as an understanding father taking in his sorry, chastened child. But when time went by and Mary stayed with Shelley, he felt less forgiving. He and his wife toughened their stance and would have nothing to do with her. The Godwins were bowing to pressure from society. They wanted to keep their other children free from the taint of disgrace. Also, with a business to run, they feared driving off disapproving customers.

Her parents' hard line pained Mary, who believed she was following Wollstonecraft's brave example. Unwilling to think that her father could take such a firm position on his own, she blamed her stepmother for swaying him. "I detest Mrs G.," she told Shelley in anger. Mary felt further hurt when Isabella, her Scottish friend, failed to answer her letters. At last a reply came from a family member who wrote that the Baxters disapproved of Mary's behavior; Isabella would not be corresponding with her. Mary sought comfort from the man she loved. "Dear good creature press me to you and hug your own Mary to your heart," she bade him.

Jane might come home, the Godwins said, if she promised to break off all contact with Mary and Shelley. She could go to the country and board with a family that had not heard her story. In this way, her reputation might still be protected. But again Jane opposed her parents; she insisted that she had done nothing shameful. Fanny bravely defied Mr. and Mrs. Godwin in her own way and made secret visits to Mary, Jane, and Shelley. She told worrisome tales of money troubles at home.

On November 30, Harriet gave birth to a son, whom she named Charles Shelley. She, too, had been ready to offer forgiveness. Instead

This sketch is of Mary Godwin at the approximate age of sixteen.

Shelley asked her for his handkerchiefs and stockings. "He cares not for me now," Harriet wrote to a friend. "He never asks after me or sends me word how he is going on. In short, the man I once loved is dead. This is a vampire." Despite the separation and change in affections, there was never a question of divorce. Divorces were rare in England in the early 1800s, and a woman had no legal right to one. A man could obtain a divorce through an act of Parliament, but this cost a great deal of money.

Shelley's law-student friend, Thomas Love Peacock.

Mary, Shelley, and Jane spent happy days that fall, giving little thought to Harriet. With the writer Thomas Peacock, they took long walks that ended at a pond where they sailed paper boats. Dark-haired, sleepy-eyed Peacock was a cheerful companion who often joined them for meals. Some days, Mary brought a book to the St. Pancras church-yard and read at her mother's grave. She would also be a mother before long; her baby was due to be born in April.

Night was the time for fire-side ghost stories. Shelley knew just what to say to arouse Jane's active imagination. It amused him to re-mind her that the clock had struck one, the "witching time of night." He then asked in an ominous voice "if it is not horrible to feel the silence of night tingling in our ears." This was enough to send Jane to her room, too frightened to sleep. Within minutes she would be back, her expression wild, insisting that her pillow had moved from the bed to the chair unaided by human hands.

Before long, Jane went too far with her show of fear. She rolled on the floor and moaned, forcing Shelley to stay up with her till dawn. Jane craved attention and might well have been pretending. She occupied an awkward position in a household with a pair of lovers who had a baby on the way, and she often felt left out.

There were two anxious weeks when Shelley hid in the home Peacock shared with his mother, leaving Mary and Jane on their own. He was avoiding the authorities who sought to lock him away in debtors' prison. According to the law, reneging on a debt was as wicked a crime as theft or fraud. If arrested, Shelley would stay behind bars until he found the means to repay what he owed. "Mary love—we must be united," Shelley wrote to her from his hideout. "My mind without yours is dead & cold as the dark midnight river when the moon is down." Mary illuminated his life, and in his poetry he compared her to the moon:

> . . . *all my being became bright or dim*
> *As the Moon's image in a summer sea,*
> *According as she smiled or frowned on me . . .*

Mary met Shelley secretly and hurriedly in dark places. She lived for Sundays, when the law forbade bailiffs from making arrests. Then he could be with her from one midnight to the next. These were days devoted to "Love in idleness," as Mary called them, days of lying in bed and talking for hours, and she savored them. "To sleep & talk—why this is merely vegetating," grumbled Jane, excluded and bored.

In January 1815, Percy's grandfather Sir Bysshe Shelley died. Feeling generous upon inheriting his father's estate, Sir Timothy rescued Percy by paying his most pressing debts. He granted Percy a yearly allowance of a thousand pounds, of which two hundred went to Harriet. Sir Timothy was less concerned about his son and daughter-in-law than about his own money and property. He hoped to stop Percy from obtaining post-obit loans, which would drain the family wealth.

Percy lied and told his father that he needed twelve hundred pounds to repay a loan from William Godwin. He then gave Godwin a thousand pounds and kept the remaining two hundred for himself. Shelley felt bound by his promise to help Godwin financially despite the older man's treatment of Mary. Godwin had no difficulty taking the money, which he believed he had as much right to as anyone else. Yet if he encountered Mary and Shelley on the street, he passed as if they were strangers.

Mary, Shelley, and Jane moved to a suburb called Hans Town, but when their landlady eyed the strange household with suspicion, they moved again, to rooms nearby. All three were feeling rundown. Shelley insisted they eat a vegetarian diet, but cabbage and root vegetables were the only produce to be had in winter.

On February 22, Mary gave birth prematurely to a girl. The child was tiny, but she nursed well, and her parents had every hope that she would live. The Godwins allowed Fanny to visit, and Charles Clairmont came on his own, bringing a gift of baby clothes. Charles was more accepting of Mary's lifestyle than his mother and stepfather were. On March 2, when the baby was nine days old, the group moved across London to roomier quarters. The wee girl was sleeping peacefully when Mary went to bed on March 5, but Mary woke on the sixth to find she had died in the night. She had never been given a name.

Mary said little and confided her feelings to her journal. "[I] think of my little dead baby," she wrote. "This is foolish I suppose; yet, whenever I am left alone to my own thoughts, and do not read to divert them, they always come back to the same point—that I was a mother, and am so no longer." Another day she recorded a dream in which she discovered that the baby was really alive, "that it had only been cold, and that we rubbed it before the fire, and it lived." Such a wish could only come true in a dream. "Awake and find no baby," Mary wrote. "I think about the little thing all day."

Life is an unsparing teacher, schooling the heart in love one day and in grief the next. Mary read many books to take her mind off her sorrow. She read works of history, biography, and philosophy. She read the New Testament, Shakespeare's plays, and popular gothic novels like *The Mysteries of Udolpho,* which tells of terrifying events in a remote castle. She read poems by her father's friend Samuel Taylor Coleridge, William Wordsworth, Lord Byron, and others.

Coleridge, Wordsworth, and Byron were poets of the Romantic movement, which celebrated freedom and the brotherhood of humanity. It was inspired by the outbreak of the French Revolution, when the common people of France rose up against tyranny. It had been fed by William Godwin's *An Enquiry Concerning Political Justice* and the writings of Mary Wollstonecraft. The Romantic poets looked to nature in its unspoiled wildness to awaken wonder and passion.

Wordsworth's poetry brought together the themes of freedom and nature:

> *How does the meadow-flower its bloom unfold?*
> *Because the lovely little flower is free*
> *Down to its root, and, in that freedom, bold.*

George Gordon, Lord Byron, was England's celebrity poet. He was witty and wise in the ways of the world. Women found him irresistible, and even men praised his looks. Coleridge went into raptures describing Byron's beautiful face: "his teeth so many stationary smiles—his eyes the open portals of the sun." Byron had large eyes and seductively long lashes, and he wore his curly hair cut short. His soft, musical speech pleased the listener's ear. A little boy who did not know Byron's name referred to him as "the gentleman with the beautiful voice." Lord Byron had been born with a malformed foot that made him walk with a limp, but he disguised his disability with a padded boot. He was an aristocrat, one of the English nobility.

Byron had taken the reading world by storm in 1812, when he published the first cantos, or sections, of his long poem *Childe Harold's Pilgrimage*. Byron's hero, Childe Harold, is a brooding, melancholy man. He turns away from a life of pleasure to travel through Spain, Portugal, and Greece. In true Romantic fashion, Childe Harold finds peace in the natural world:

> *To climb the trackless mountain all unseen,*
> *With the wild flock that never needs a fold;*
>
> . . . .
>
> *This is not solitude; 'tis but to hold*
> *Converse with Nature's charms, and view her*
> *stores unroll'd.*

The knowledge Mary gained from reading made her a strong debater. Her sharp mind intrigued Shelley's college friend Thomas Jefferson Hogg. He drew her into friendly arguments on subjects such as virtue and free will. The discussions distracted Mary from her loss, which Shelley was glad to see.

"Mary's illness disappears for a time," he noted. Hogg never could win these verbal contests, so after a while he gave up and joined the others in telling nighttime ghost stories. Hogg had large, solid features; few people would have called him handsome. He could be loud and brash. But he was fond of Mary and may have fancied that he loved her. About his ever-more-frequent visits, Mary said, "I like him better each time."

Samuel Taylor Coleridge,
a friend of the Godwins,
is remembered as one of the
important Romantic poets.

The poetry and
notorious personal life of
George Gordon, Lord Byron,
had made him a celebrity.

Mary wanted a break from the constant presence of another person: Jane. Her stepsister had been Percy's companion for walks and shopping trips when pregnancy and mourning kept Mary housebound. Mary could see that Percy liked Jane's high spirits and enchanting dark eyes, maybe a little too much. But even he was growing tired of her childish outbursts. He used some of the money received from his father to send her away to the seaside village of Lynmouth, where she stayed in a pretty cottage under the eye of a prudent landlady. Jane changed her name to Claire—Claire Clairmont—which sounded glamorous to her ears.

On their own for the first time, Mary and Shelley went in late spring to another picturesque coastal town, Torquay. The English believed the sea air at Torquay was especially healthy to breathe. Mary filled her lungs, inhaling all its goodness. She was going to have another baby and was doing all she could to take care of herself and her unborn child.

That summer, Shelley found a new home west of London for himself and Mary. It was a two-story brick cottage near Windsor Great Park, the thousands of acres stretching south from the king's residence, Windsor Castle. Against this sweeping green background, Mary tended flowers, read, and studied Latin. Shelley sat against a tree in the royal park, writing poetry. In this setting, he composed a lengthy poem titled *Alastor*.

Shelley tended to write long poems; he liked to expand on his ideas for many lines rather than pare them down into brief verses. In *Alastor*, a poet journeys to imaginary lands seeking an ideal love, a "veilèd maid" who sat near him in a dream. "Her voice was like the voice of his own soul," Shelley wrote. Perhaps she was a symbol for poetic inspiration. Published in 1816 along with some of his other poetry, *Alastor* was the first important poem by Percy Shelley that

Percy Shelley wrote poetry under the chestnut trees in Windsor Forest.

the public had a chance to read. Mary saw in it "the worship of the majesty of Nature, the broodings of a poet's heart in solitude."

In September, joined by Peacock and Mary's stepbrother, Charles Clairmont, Mary and Shelley went for a boat trip on the Thames. They rode north, hoping to reach the river's source. The ten-day excursion took them to Oxford, where Shelley showed the others the rooms where he and Hogg had lived. Rowing on past chalky hills, woodlands, and rolling farms, the friends talked of many things, from the government to the benefit and harm of a vegetarian diet. Peacock had convinced Shelley to eat some well-peppered mutton chops before they left, believing they would boost the poet's stamina.

For Mary and Shelley, nature did have the power to heal, as the Romantic poets had promised. They imagined what it would be like to keep going, to wend their way by river and canal to distant parts of England. "Shelley even proposed, in his wildness, that there should be no halting-place," Charles Clairmont informed his sister Claire. Shelley envisioned a trip through Wales and Scotland, "when by the time we returned we should have voyaged two thousand miles," wrote twenty-year-old Charles. But when they reached a spot where the Thames had grown shallow and wading cows blocked their progress, they turned around and rowed home.

Autumn passed contentedly into winter, and on January 24, 1816, Mary gave birth to a healthy boy. Now, holding her small son, Mary learned the joy of seeing a child of hers thrive. She and Shelley named the baby William, after Mary's father. They hoped this gesture might persuade William Godwin to accept them into the family circle, but they were in for a rude surprise. Not only did Godwin remain as firmly disapproving as ever, but he had the nerve to bother Shelley for more money. This time Shelley shot back an angry letter chiding Godwin for being "thus harsh and cruel."

And what was Claire up to all this time? Bored in Lynmouth, she had returned to Skinner Street, to keep her mother company while William Godwin went to Edinburgh on business. Mr. and Mrs. Godwin still hoped to bring her back into the family fold. Claire was restless, though, and wanted more from life. She dreamed of being someone people noticed, an actress or a playwright. To succeed, she needed help, so she wrote a letter to the most famous person she could think of, the poet Lord Byron.

Byron was now at the center of a shocking scandal. Recently separated from his wife, he was rumored to have had an incestuous affair with his half sister. One of his lovers called him "mad, bad, and dangerous to know." Any girl trying to salvage her reputation was wise to stay far away from him, but Claire believed she was not just any girl. She was a disciple of Mary Wollstonecraft and a talent waiting to be discovered. Besides, Byron was on the board of the Drury Lane Theatre, where the greatest actors performed.

Claire's letter gained her a brief, unpromising interview. Unwilling to be ignored, she kept on writing to Byron. She sent him stories she had written. She told him that she scorned marriage and hinted that she was an atheist. She revealed that she was connected to William Godwin, whom Byron admired, and his daughter with Wollstonecraft, Mary. She said, too, that she was close to an unknown poet of genius. Her letters charmed Byron, who met with her again. Pretty soon, sure

The only known portrait of Claire Clairmont was painted in 1819 by Amelia Curran, who had known the Godwins for many years.

she had made a conquest, Claire offered herself to him. Together they could take a coach out of town, "about the distance of ten or twelve miles," she wrote. "There we shall be free and unknown; we can return early the following morning." Claire was not quite eighteen years old; Byron was twenty-eight.

As Byron's mistress, Claire sat with him in his private box at the theater. He wrote verses in praise of her singing: "like music on the waters / Is thy sweet voice to me . . ." Claire brought Mary to meet Byron but insisted he keep their sexual intimacy secret. "Mary is delighted with you as I knew she would be," Claire wrote to him afterward.

Byron left London in April 1816, to escape the city's gossip peddlers. He was headed for Geneva, Switzerland, and he was going without Claire. She knew he felt no love for her. "Were I to float by your window drowned all you would say would be 'Ah voila!'" she wrote to him. Yet she was not about to let her poet slip away. Claire suggested to Mary and Shelley that they all go to Geneva too. Mary and Shelley were eager to get out of England, where they lived a nearly friendless life, and where Shelley owed money. Shelley also was excited to think he might get to know Byron. So in early May, they set off with baby William on another European adventure.

CHAPTER FOUR

Year Without a Summer

*I busied myself to think of a story ... one to make the
reader dread to look round, to curdle the blood, and
quicken the beatings of the heart.*

They registered at the Hôtel d'Angleterre, a place popular with
English tourists, as a married couple traveling with the wife's
sister. Claire knew that Byron planned to stop at this hotel after he
did some sightseeing, and she wanted to be waiting when he arrived.

Until he came, Mary, Shelley, and Claire filled their days with
walks on the hotel grounds, watching rabbits nibbling on flowers
and little lizards darting across their path. The surrounding foot-
hills and mountains reminded Mary of Scotland. Shelley rented
a boat, and they sailed on Lake Geneva. "The lovely lake," Mary
called it, "blue as the heavens which it reflects, and sparkling with
golden beams." She leaned her head back and let the wind blow
through her hair. With William plump and strong, Mary felt deep
happiness. Sometimes she laughed out loud in pure joy. She and
Shelley hired a Swiss woman named Elise Duvillard to help with

William's care. Elise was a few years older than Mary and Shelley. Unmarried, she had a daughter who was being raised by her parents.

Two weeks later, Byron drove up in splendid style, in a coach that he had ordered built. Painted a bold blue with gold and red stripes, it looked like one of Napoleon's. He came with a friend, a twenty-one-year-old physician named John Polidori, and brought along a dog, a monkey, and a peacock. For a day and a half, Byron avoided Claire and her party, but when he encountered them on the beach, he greeted them as good manners required. It was a fortunate meeting: Byron and Shelley liked each other from the start and quickly became friends. Polidori admired Mary and soon began teaching her to speak Italian.

The hotel was filled with nosy guests who had spotted the illustrious newcomer. Byron called them "a parcel of staring boobies." To escape their gawking, he rented a villa a mile away, not far from the pretty town of Cologny. Shelley, Mary, and Claire leased a more modest house nearby. It was close enough to the villa for Claire to see who came and went. When Polidori stepped out, she sneaked over and slipped into Byron's bed.

Not to be outsmarted, curious English tourists boarded boats and sailed past Cologny, eager to spot proof of Byron's debauchery. They let their imaginations run wild, insisting that bedsheets hanging on his clothesline were women's petticoats. Shaking their heads, they told one another that the poet was running a bordello. An Englishman wrote home to report that Byron had taken up with a "family of very suspicious appearance. How many he has at his disposal out of the whole set I know not." One hotel owner brought in a telescope so his guests could spy on the alluring group from the comfort of his rooms.

Shelley deplored this attitude, which he labeled "social hatred."

To escape prying eyes, Byron and Polidori holed up in the Villa Diodati.
Mary, Shelley, and Claire rented a house nearby.

There were English people, he observed, who detested "those whose conduct and opinions are not precisely modelled on their own. The systems of those ideas forms a superstition, which constantly demands and constantly finds fresh victims."

He and his companions simply wanted to enjoy their holiday. They rode horses and mules into the Jura Mountains, following rutted paths left by carriage wheels. They explored medieval castles. Mary, Shelley, and Claire went to Chamonix, a pretty village beside the river Arve. Mary watched this rushing mountain waterway crash against its banks "like a wild animal who is furious in constraint." She wandered in alpine meadows, collecting wildflower seeds that she hoped to plant in a garden one day.

Chamonix sits at the base of Mont Blanc, the highest Alpine peak. The mountain's strength and silence awed Shelley and inspired him to write a poem. "All things that move and breathe with toil and sound / Are born and die," he wrote. Meanwhile, "Mont Blanc

A standing Byron recites for his friends as they boat on Lake Geneva. The two ladies are Mary and Claire. Shelley sits in the stern, and John Polidori balances at the side of the craft. The two oarsmen have been hired for the outing.

yet gleams on high." The mountain appears eternal, part of "the everlasting universe of things."

Later in the poem, he observes, "In the lone glare of day, the snows descend." Contemplating that mountaintop snow, Shelley finds a power in himself. After all, how could nature's beauty exist without a thinking being to perceive it? He asks the mountain,

> *And what were thou, and earth, and stars, and sea,*
> *If to the human mind's imaginings*
> *Silence and solitude were vacancy?*

Shelley could be starry-eyed and impulsive, but he could also write beautiful, complex poetry.

There were many days that June when rain and chill kept everyone indoors. People called 1816 "the year without a summer." Around the globe, temperatures stayed two or three degrees below average. The change was enough to cause heavy snowfalls in the northeastern United States in late spring and crop failures in Europe and India. The strange weather resulted from the explosion of Mount Tambora, in Indonesia, more than a year before. This volcanic eruption—the largest in recorded history—sent millions of tons of dust and ash high into the atmosphere. Much of it fell to Earth, killing many thousands of people in the region, but the tiniest particles stayed aloft. Air currents carried them over the Northern Hemisphere, where they absorbed sunlight and disrupted normal

Majestic Mont Blanc rises behind the village of Chamonix.

weather patterns and people's lives. At the time, no one understood the connection between the catastrophic event in Asia and changes in the climate thousands of miles away. People blamed the strange weather on sunspots, earthquakes in the Lower Mississippi Valley, or simply God's will.

On stormy nights, the friends gathered at Byron's villa. As thunder boomed overhead and sheets of rain washed down the long balcony windows, Mary and the others sat in the warmth and comfort of a roaring fire. They stayed up late into the night, talking over strange occurrences and novel ideas. One night, John Polidori read aloud his notes from a lecture by Sir William Lawrence, a surgeon whose teachings were causing controversy. Lawrence claimed that human consciousness arose solely from the workings of the brain. God played no role, and there was no such thing as a soul. "I see the animal functions inseparable from the animal organs," he professed.

The next night, Byron read from an old book of eerie tales that an earlier tenant had left behind at the villa. In one, a ghostly barber is condemned to haunt the castle where he plied his trade in life. In another, the stolen head of a corpse is made to live again. His friends' fascination with the nature of life and their enjoyment of these bizarre accounts gave Byron an idea. "We will each write a ghost-story," he said. Immediately, everyone was excited. Writing their stories would be fun and a perfect way to stay busy on rainy days.

Mary searched her mind for an idea, but she came up with nothing. Feeling frustrated, she lay in bed one night, her thoughts too active for sleep. It was well after the witching hour when, to her astonishment, a story suddenly emerged from her imagination. One image after another arose before her, "with shut eyes, but acute mental vision," as she later wrote. Her mind revealed a character and the

A German artist tried to convey the enormity of the 1816 explosion of Mount Tambora. This massive volcanic eruption affected the planet's weather for years.

unsavory work he had underway. "I saw the pale student of unhallowed arts kneeling beside the thing he had put together. I saw the hideous phantasm of a man stretched out, and then, on the working of some powerful engine, show signs of life." The student is attempting an experiment like the ones Mary and her friends had discussed, bringing dead tissue to life. He is building a horrifying, manlike creature—a monster he will release into the world. The story had come, vivid and unbidden, from the depths of Mary's unconscious. "A thrill of fear ran through me," she recalled. She opened her eyes and sought calm in the moonlight filtering through closed shutters onto the parquet floor and other familiar details of real life.

"What terrified me will terrify others," Mary knew. In the morning, she told her story to the rest of the group, all enthusiastic listeners. Shelley thought she should expand it into a novel. "But for his incitement it would never have taken the form in which it was presented to the world," Mary later said. Through July and August, while the others merely toyed with their stories, Mary worked steadily. By summer's end, she had completed a rough draft of her book about the student, whom she named Victor Frankenstein, and the being he endows with life.

Meanwhile, letters came from England, among them one from Shelley's father's lawyer. Sir Timothy offered to raise Percy's allowance by five hundred pounds, and lend him another two thousand, if Percy returned to England. Sir Timothy was furious at Percy for leaving the country without providing proper support for Harriet, Ianthe, and Charles. He wanted his flighty son to come home and take care of his dependents. Another letter came from Fanny, who wrote to say that the bookshop was losing money, and that trying to make ends meet was stressing the Godwin household. Sad to be missing out on the fun the others were having, Fanny begged for tidbits about Byron. Mary and Shelley sent a gold watch to Fanny, who so often seemed depressed.

Claire had something to say, but not to Fanny. She announced to the circle of friends that she was having a baby. In fact, she was already carrying Byron's child before she left England. By this time, Byron had tired of Claire. "I never loved nor pretended to love her," he wrote to a friend in England, "but a man is a man—& if a girl of eighteen comes prancing to you at all hours—there is but one way." He said, however, that he would recognize the child as his own after it was born and raise it himself in Europe. Claire would be allowed to see her daughter or son, but she was to act the role of a visiting aunt.

They may sound odd and coldhearted today, but those were actually generous terms, and Claire had to accept them. British law protected men's right to custody of their children but not women's. Byron could have excluded Claire from her child's life altogether. He had the financial means to provide well for a child, and he wanted his son or daughter raised apart from the wandering, atheistic Shelleys.

The law also required men to support their illegitimate children, but this provision was weakly enforced. Many desperate single mothers had no choice but to leave their babies on a church doorstep, knowing the parish provided for orphans whose relatives were unknown. Others farmed their children out, paying a fee to a broker who promised to place the babe in a competent person's care. These brokers were unscrupulous, though. Farmed-out children were often drugged and fed watered-down milk, and they tended to die at an early age. Yet a woman knew that if she wanted to live a respectable life, she could not carry the shame of an illegitimate child.

Driven from her home and thrown upon the world, an unwed mother carries her child through foul weather.

Showing great kindness, Shelley said that he would support and look after Claire until Byron took over responsibility for his child. Feeling the weight of all the people depending on him, Shelley wrote a will. He left the bulk of his estate to Mary Godwin. His wife, Harriet, was to receive six thousand pounds, and the children Ianthe and Charles would get five thousand each. Shelley willed six thousand pounds to Claire; he set aside another six thousand pounds to help support her child. He also left sums to his friends Peacock, Hogg, and Byron. Of course, this document was more a wish list than a will. Shelley possessed none of this money, although he expected to inherit it one day.

More than before, Shelley needed the funds he would get from his father by returning to England. So on August 29, Mary said goodbye to the beautiful lake. "I shall ever love thee," she wrote.

She had looked forward to a home life without Claire's constant presence, but because of the pregnancy, she would have to wait. She agreed to stand by her stepsister and offer help and emotional support. Claire sent a note to Byron at his villa. "I shall love you to the end of my life & nobody else," she wrote, but Byron never replied. Mary, Claire, and Shelley left for home with seven-month-old William and his Swiss nursemaid, Elise Duvillard.

They went to Bath, a city where they knew no one, to wait out the next few months. With Claire posing as "Mrs. Clairmont," they hoped to get her through the crisis of pregnancy and childbirth while keeping her reputation clean. This was why they informed the Godwins that Claire was unwell, and that she was in Bath to drink water from its natural springs, which were said to promote health.

William and Mary Jane Godwin asked no questions. Another daughter worried them more. It seems that Fanny had slipped away from Skinner Street, and no one knew where she had gone. On October 9, Mary received a dark, distressing letter from her older sister that hinted of suicide. Shelley rushed to Bristol, the city where the letter was postmarked, but he had no luck finding Fanny. The Godwins, too, received an ill-boding letter, and William Godwin made his own fruitless search.

News, when it came, could not have been worse. Fanny's body had been discovered in a room at an inn in the Welsh port of Swansea. She had taken her own life by swallowing laudanum. The note she left stated that she had decided to "put an end to the existence of a being whose birth was unfortunate, and whose life has only been a series of pain to those persons who have hurt their health in endeavouring to promote her welfare." On her wrist she wore the gold watch from Mary and Shelley.

Claire awaited her baby's birth in the resort city of Bath.
Ancient Romans once bathed in the region's mineral-rich water.

Suicide was a crime in the early nineteenth century and a source of shame for surviving families. Many people considered it an evil act that made a soul unfit to enter Heaven. The spirits of people who took their own lives were said to suffer torment. The Godwins knew better, but even in their grief, they stayed away from Swansea. They ordered their other children, Claire, Charles, William—and Mary—to do the same. No one outside the family was to know what Fanny had done. "My advice and earnest prayer is that you would avoid anything that leads to publicity," Mr. Godwin wrote in the first letter he sent to Mary since she ran off with Shelley. He and his wife told people outside the family that Fanny had gone to Ireland and died there of a fever. She was buried in an unmarked grave.

The survivors struggled to make sense of her suicide. In Skinner Street, William Godwin convinced himself that Fanny had been secretly in love with Shelley, and that this was why she chose to die. Mary, still estranged from her father and stepmother, confessed to feeling miserable and full of regret. If only she had done more to include Fanny in her life! If only Fanny had held on until Claire's baby was born and away in Byron's care! "My house would then have been a proper asylum for her," Mary lamented. The sad truth is that Fanny had no clear reason for ending her life. She likely suffered from what today would be diagnosed as clinical depression, a condition that can put people at risk for suicide.

For Fanny's grieving family, life had to go on. Dressed in black mourning clothes, Mary took drawing lessons and went to lectures on books and philosophy. There were weeks when Shelley was away. He was looking, without luck, for a house they might dwell in after Claire's confinement. When he was in Bath, Mary strolled with him and baby William alongside stylish vacationers. She took in a pair of cats. Mary also worked on her novel, revising her first draft so the story flowed logically and smoothly. In the evening, Shelley read aloud to Mary and Claire. He described the tranquil scene at home in a letter to Byron, who was on his way to Venice. "Mary is reading over the fire; our cat and kitten are sleeping under the sofa; and little Willy is just gone to sleep." Claire, he noted, "is writing to you at this instant." Claire still hoped to revive Byron's interest in her.

The serenity lasted only a short while. On December 15, Shelley received an upsetting letter informing him that Harriet was dead. A friend in London had written that in September Harriet had left her children at her father's house and moved into rooms near soldiers' quarters, using the name Harriet Smith. On November 9, she went missing. On December 10, she was found dead in the Serpentine, a lake in London's Hyde Park, in an advanced state of pregnancy. No one knows exactly what happened, but Harriet may have been abandoned by an army officer with whom she had had an affair; she appeared to have drowned herself. Once, Harriet had described her time with Shelley as "the happiest and *longest* two years" of her life. Now, because she was a suicide, neither Shelley nor Harriet's family claimed her remains.

Shelley's thoughts were of his motherless children, Ianthe and Charles. He barely knew them, but he wanted them to come and live with him. Mary, he believed, would be a tender mother to them, just as she was to William. And Mary was ready to welcome them into her arms. "How very happy shall I be to possess those darling treasures that are yours," she told Shelley. By tradition and law, a widower had custody of his minor children, but Harriet's parents, the Westbrooks, were claiming the right to be the legal guardians of the little girl and boy they loved. They filed a suit against Shelley in chancery court, alleging that his atheism, radical ideas, and relationship with Mary made him an unfit parent. Chancery court handled cases involving the distribution of property and the guardianship of children. Its judges sought to be impartial and fair, sometimes relying on good sense as much as the word of law. Months might pass until the case of Ianthe and Charles was decided; until then, the children were ordered to stay with the Westbrooks.

Harriet's death left Shelley free to remarry, and he believed he would appear more responsible to the court if Mary were his wife. Mary had her own reason for wanting marriage. If she and Shelley were legally wed, she thought, her father's attitude toward them might soften. As it turned out, she was right. When Mary Wollstonecraft Godwin and Percy Bysshe Shelley married, on December 30, 1816, at London's St. Mildred's Church, William and Mary Jane Godwin witnessed the ceremony.

"You can scarcely imagine how great a relief this has brought to mine and Mrs. Godwin's mind," Mr. Godwin wrote to William Baxter in Scotland. Mary, he continued, had "acquired a status and character in society." He praised Shelley's "many good and even noble qualities." William Godwin painted a rosy picture of Mary's life, doing his best to present it as respectable. But like most of society, Baxter was less willing than Mary's father to overlook her actions during the past two and a half years, and Isabella was still forbidden to have contact with her.

Mary Godwin and Percy Shelley were married in St. Mildred's Church on December 30, 1816.

In this way, the year without a summer came to an end. Mary was now a mother and wife. She had written a novel that she hoped to see published. These joys, however, had been tempered by a dark season that brought the deaths of Fanny and Harriet.

Would the coming year begin on a note of hope? The answer was yes. On January 13, 1817, Mary sent a letter to Byron, telling him that Claire "was safely delivered of a little girl yesterday morning." Claire named her daughter Alba. The letters *lb* in the baby girl's name stood for Lord Byron. "It is a long time since Shelley has heard from you and I am sure nothing would give him greater pleasure than to hear news of your motions & enjoyments," Mary wrote. More time would pass, though, until his friends in England received word from Byron.

CHAPTER FIVE

Dreams

While there is life there is action and change. We go on...

In December 1816, a newspaper editor named Leigh Hunt singled out Percy Shelley as "a very striking and original thinker." Most critics had ignored *Alastor* because they disapproved of Shelley's atheism and sensational private life. But Hunt had read the long poem, and he spotted genius in its lines. He began corresponding with the poet, and soon the Hunts and Shelleys became friends. Hunt and his wife, Marianne, had no qualms about welcoming the couple who had been the focus of so much scandalous talk.

Mary Shelley felt drawn to the Hunts and their burgeoning family. There were four Hunt children when the couples met, and there would be ten in all. They served as models for their mother, who was a sculptor. Marianne Hunt was a big, hearty woman whom it was easy to like. Leigh Hunt had dark hair and full, soft cheeks.

Editor Leigh Hunt was
an early champion of
Percy Shelley's poetry.

The woman
in this sketch is
thought to be
Marianne Hunt.

He often lounged around the house in his dressing gown, thinking and writing about art and beauty.

Leigh Hunt was known for speaking his mind in print. If he found fault with the actions of Parliament or a national figure, he fearlessly published his opinion. One steady reader praised his paper, the *Examiner*, for its "liberty-loving, liberty-advocating, liberty-eloquent articles." In March 1812, Hunt had criticized the prince regent. The prince—the future King George IV—was reigning in place of his father, King George III, who was mentally ill. Everyone knew that the prince regent had a mistress and lived beyond his means, but to ridicule him in the press amounted to slander. Hunt, however, had called the prince an aging, overweight "Adonis" and a "libertine over head and ears in debt and disgrace." For this he had earned two years in jail.

Leigh Hunt was not the only Englishman to criticize the prince regent in print. This political cartoon contrasts the regent's lavish lifestyle with the poverty that many of his subjects endured.

Leigh Hunt, who played the piano and had a pleasing voice, invited the Shelleys to come over for musical evenings. The Shelleys also went with the Hunts to concerts and the theater. One night at an opera, Leigh Hunt observed Mary as she gave all her attention to the stage. He saw a thoughtful, "sedate-faced young lady" with a "great tablet of a forehead." Mary could be too serious, in Hunt's view. He preferred to see her in playful conversation, when he nicknamed her "nymph of the sidelong looks."

Shelley often looked at Mary too. He paid tribute to her in verse:

> *in the paleness of thy thoughtful cheek,*
> *And in the light thine ample forehead wears,*
> *And in thy sweetest smiles, and in thy tears,*
> *And in thy gentle speech, a prophecy*
> *Is whispered, to subdue my fondest fears . . .*

The woman with the sweet smiles was pregnant again. She and Shelley dreamed of a home in England where they could settle down and raise their family. Shelley signed a twenty-one-year lease on a house in Marlow, a town west of London, on the Thames. Albion House was a white-painted structure that stood outside the village. The Shelleys moved in on March 18, 1817; Claire and Alba joined them a week later. Claire had been living in rooms nearby and waiting for word from Byron. Since losing Fanny, Mary felt renewed affection for her stepsister and tried to be more accepting of Claire. Both women had young children and shared the concerns of motherhood.

Spring brought brightness and warmth to Marlow, and summer, long missing, returned. Mary planted her alpine seeds in a tidy garden. Albion House "is very comfortable and expectant of its promised guests," she wrote to the Hunts. "Come then, dear, good creatures, and let us enjoy with you the beauty of the Marlow sun." Marlow was close enough to London for the Hunts and William Godwin to visit easily. A zealous hiker could even walk the distance, as Shelley sometimes did.

In a burst of energy, Shelley purchased new furniture for Albion House and had old pieces reupholstered. He stocked the spacious library with books and graced it with statues of Apollo and Venus— the Greek sun god and the Roman goddess of love. Relying on credit because he had spent his allowance, he bought a piano for Claire. In his generosity, Shelley loaned cash to his friends. He also handed out coins, blankets, and clothing to Marlow's poor. Once, after giving his shoes to a needy man, he walked back to Albion House barefoot. The people of Marlow grew used to the sight of slim, slouching

The Shelleys moved into Albion House, thinking that they would settle there for a long time.

Percy Shelley tapping on the doors of humble cottages, tramping off with a notebook to compose poems in the woods, or heading home with burrs sticking to his long brown coat.

Mary was writing too. She put the finishing touches on *Frankenstein* and sent it to a London publisher. This firm rejected it, and so did another. The story was too bizarre, Mary was told; readers would find it too unsettling. Mary disagreed. Confident that her book would find an audience, she mailed it to a third publisher. While she waited for a response, Mary felt warmed by glowing comments from her father, who had read her manuscript. William Godwin called *Frankenstein* "the most wonderful work to have been written at twenty years of age that I ever heard of." (Mary was actually nineteen when she completed her novel.)

She also went through the journal she and Shelley had kept in 1814, when they first ran off to Europe, with the idea of transforming it into a book. She polished the writing and added letters she and Percy had written to Fanny and Peacock in 1816, while in Geneva. Percy tacked on his poem "Mont Blanc." Travel books were popular at the time. Photography had yet to be invented, and usually just the wealthy or adventurous went abroad. Reading a book was the only way for many people to know what it was like to tour Italy or venture into deepest Africa. Books transported them to the forests surrounding St. Petersburg, Russia, or the villages of distant Persia. Mary Wollstonecraft had taken her readers to Scandinavia with her book *Letters Written during a Short Residence in Sweden, Norway, and Denmark*.

The Shelleys' book, *History of a Six Weeks' Tour through a Part of France, Switzerland, Germany, and Holland*, earned a few good reviews in the press. One book critic noted that it contained "little information, no reflection, and very few incidents . . . yet it somehow of his science. ~~Bes~~ Besides I had a contempt for the uses of modern ~~chemistry~~ natural philosophy. It was very ~~~~ different when ~~the~~ masters of the science sought immortality and ~~health~~ power; such views although futile were grand; but now the scene was ~~all~~ changed. ~~and the ex~~ ~~of chimera~~ overthrown ~~at the~~ ~~all~~ ~~greatness in the science~~. Such were my reflections during the two or three days I spent almost in ~~~~ solitude: but ~~at~~ as the ensuing week commenced I thought of the information M. Krempe had given me concerning the lectures. and although I could not consent to go and hear that little conceited fellow deliver sentences out of a pulpit, I recollected what he had said of M. Waldman, whom I had never seen ~~and~~ as he had been hitherto out of town.

Partly ~~~~ from curiosity and partly from idleness I went into the lecturing room which M. Waldman entered shortly after. This professor was a very different man from ~~the other~~ his colleague. He was about fifty but with aspect expressive of the greatest benevolence a few grey ~~hairs~~ hairs covered his temples

the extent of enquirer seemed to limit itself to the annihilation of those visions on which

My interest in science was chiefly founded. I was required to exchange chimeras of boundless grandeur for realities of little worth.

or other produces considerable amusement and interest." No author's name appeared on the book, but the critic understood that it had been written mostly by a "Lady." "She prattles away very prettily," he commented. "Now and then a French phrase drops sweetly enough from her fair mouth." He was condescending toward the woman author, but he also offered some praise: "Her heart is at all times open to gladness and kindly feeling; and we think that no one will part with so amiable and agreeable a companion, without regret, and sincere wishes for her future happiness." Despite the good words for the book, only a small number of copies sold.

On September 2, 1817, Mary gave birth to a daughter she and Percy named Clara. Clara was a fussy newborn, and Mary grew exhausted soothing her day and night. She watched anxiously over nineteen-month-old William as well, lest he catch a chill as the weather turned cool. Money problems also wore at Mary's nerves. Debts were piling up again, and her father continued to pressure Shelley for help with his own financial troubles.

In November, good news came just when Mary needed it. *Frankenstein* had found a publisher. Lackington, Allen and Company printed books with such spooky titles as *Apparitions; or, The Mystery of Ghosts, Hobgoblins, and Haunted Houses* and *Tales of the Dead.* The firm also ran a popular shop called the Temple of the Muses, where books lined the walls from floor to ceiling. Like many novels of the time, especially those written by women, *Frankenstein* would be published anonymously.

But bad tidings came on the heels of good. In autumn, the chancery court reached a decision on the guardianship of Ianthe and Charles Shelley. Neither their father nor the Westbrooks were to have custody of the children. Instead the little ones were sent to

Books cover the walls in the Temple of the Muses, the bookshop run by Lackington, Allen and Company, the firm that published *Frankenstein*. Many more books are shelved in the upstairs balcony.

live with court-appointed foster parents, an esteemed minister and his wife.

No one had expected this outcome. The court's ruling threw Percy Shelley into a panic. He feared—for no good reason—that the authorities might snatch William and Clara away from him. He was so distressed that he came down with imaginary illnesses. After sitting in a coach beside a woman with heavy legs, he worried that he had caught elephantiasis, a rare disease that causes great swelling. For weeks he checked his legs for any sign of enlargement. As the days grew short and Albion House became chilly and damp, Shelley was certain that the changing weather was harming his health. Surely he would waste away unless he moved to a warm place— somewhere like Italy, where Byron was living.

The Shelleys and Claire still had heard nothing from Byron; a new love affair was taking up his time. They told people that Alba was the child of London friends who had sent her into the country for her health. Living with a lie can be tricky, though, and to honest people, it can simply feel wrong. So pretty soon the residents of Albion House admitted that Alba was Claire's daughter. Once that happened, the local gentry made up their own lie, that Percy was Alba's real father. They pointed fingers at Mary, Percy, and Claire and avoided their company. "Country town friends are not very agreeable," Mary commented dryly.

At long last, Byron wrote to ask that his daughter be baptized in the Church of England and given the name Allegra; he mentioned nothing about taking over her care. Perhaps it would be wise to bring Allegra to her father, Shelley reasoned. Byron could afford to support her, and without the day-to-day responsibility of a child, Claire could find work as a lady's companion or governess. The decision was made: they would all go to Italy. The Shelleys sold off many of their possessions. Percy found a new tenant to take over the lease on Albion House and obtained another post-obit loan. Recklessly generous as always, he gave half the money to Leigh Hunt, who was short of funds, and a hundred and fifty pounds to Mary's father. William Godwin had wanted more, and he let the Shelleys know he was displeased.

Mary was eager to leave. Her impossible father, lenders demanding to be repaid, a prudish society, Percy's wavering health—sailing to Europe meant leaving them all behind. *"Le rêve est fini,"* she wrote in her journal; the dream of English country life had ended.

On March 9, 1818, all three children were baptized. Allegra was fourteen months old. Mary had nicknamed her "the little Commodore" for the comical way she stood on her sturdy legs and stared at adults as though she were the one in charge. William had turned two in January, and Clara was just six months old. Percy Shelley hoped that baptizing William and Clara might silence any imaginary foes who considered him an unfit parent.

On March 13, a year after they moved to Marlow, the Shelleys left England. Eight people traveled together: Mary, Percy, Claire, the three children, Elise Duvillard, and Milly Shields, a local girl who had been hired to help Elise. They sailed from Dover to France, where they purchased a carriage and hired a driver to take them over the Alps. After a stop in Switzerland, where Elise saw her daughter, they ascended a snowy mountain pass. Elated to be on the move, Percy sang all the way, his voice echoing off cliffs and frozen waterfalls. The rocky peaks, he said, were God's ballet dancers.

The travelers stayed at an inn in the northern Italian city of Milan. Tourists flocked to Milan to gaze at Leonardo da Vinci's famous painting *The Last Supper*, in the Convent of Santa Maria delle Grazie. Moisture had damaged the work since Leonardo completed it in 1498, but Mary was thrilled to see it nonetheless. She liked everything about Milan and the countryside around it, "the fruit trees all in blossom and the fields green with the growing corn." Pulling the peasants' carts were "the most beautiful oxen I ever saw," she wrote. "They are of a delicate dove colour."

Mary and Shelley dreamed now of making a life for their family in Italy. They talked about renting a house beside beautiful Lake Como, so deep, blue, and serene. Percy wrote to Byron in Venice, inviting him to spend the summer nearby. This would give everyone time to discuss Allegra's future, Shelley said. Ideally she could grow up knowing both her parents, even if she saw them under different roofs. Byron replied that he was not interested in such an arrangement. He would not be coming to Lake Como, and he was sending

Milan's cathedral, with its many spires.

a messenger to fetch his daughter. He had no wish to see Claire, then or ever. Claire's bond with Allegra was to be permanently broken, just like that.

How could Byron do such a thing? Claire was torn apart. Desperate to change his mind, she dashed off a frantic note, writing too swiftly to bother with punctuation. "My dear Lord Byron I most truly love my child," she pleaded. "She loves me she stretches out her arms to me & cooes for joy when I take her." Claire had wept so much, she added, "that now my eyes seem to drop hot & burning blood." Percy kept his feelings under control as he composed a pointed letter of his own. Claire, he noted, "requires reassurance and tenderness. A tie so near to the heart should not be rudely snapt." He continued, "Your conduct must at present wear the aspect of great cruelty, however you justify it to yourself." Shelley managed to accomplish a little good. Byron sent assurances that he would take good care of Allegra, and that Claire might visit her in the summer.

Claire was in a sorry situation and wretchedly sad. She wanted to keep Allegra with her, but it was out of the question. It would mean depending indefinitely on Shelley for support, and she dared not ask that. Also, she needed to seek a job, and this was impossible to do with a child in tow. Claire knew that Byron could raise their daughter in comfort, but the thought of seeing Allegra only in summer devastated her.

Byron's messenger showed up in late April. He was Francis Merriweather, an Englishman who ran a shop in Venice. Claire searched her mind for a reason—any reason—to delay him. Allegra was sick, too sick to travel, she said. But the little girl's healthy glow made it plain that this was untrue. At last, Mary came up with a way to help Claire say goodbye. Suppose Elise Duvillard went to Venice too, Mary suggested. Elise could care for Allegra and help her get settled, and she would be a familiar face among strangers. She could also inform Claire about her child's well-being. Claire said she could live with that arrangement, so on April 28, the day after Claire's birthday, Allegra and Elise left with Merriweather.

Soon Elise wrote to say that Allegra had reached Venice safely and was being looked after well. "They dress her in little trousers trimmed with lace & treat her like a little princess," Mary informed the Hunts. Elise and Allegra moved into the home of Richard Hoppner, the British consul in Venice, and his wife. Byron had wanted custody of Allegra, but he had arranged for her to live apart from him, with other people looking after her. Claire dreamed of August, when she would go to Venice and see her daughter again.

Meanwhile, Lake Como was forgotten. Mary and Shelley went with their children, Claire, and Milly Shields to Pisa, where Mary climbed all two hundred and twenty-four steps to the top of the famous Leaning Tower. She looked down on the neighboring cathedral square, where the sight of prisoners in chains cleaning the pavement made her reflect sadly on the people throughout the world who were enslaved.

From Pisa they made the short trip to Livorno, a city on the Ligurian Sea. There they called on someone Mary had known years before. She was Maria Reveley, who had cared for Mary in infancy. After her husband's death, Reveley had married John Gisborne, a businessman, and moved with him to Italy. Known now as Mrs. Gisborne, she welcomed the newcomers and spoke fondly of William Godwin and Mary Wollstonecraft. The Shelleys admired Gisborne's mastery of painting and European languages and her fearless atheism. "She is reserved, yet with easy manners," Mary noted in her journal. She wrote to her father, "How inexpressibly pleasing it is to call back the recollection of years long past, and especially when the recollection belongs to a person in whom one deeply interested oneself."

Mary and Percy also enjoyed seeing Maria Gisborne's son Henry Reveley. Fanny's old playmate was twenty-eight and studying to be an engineer. He dreamed of building a steamboat powerful enough to carry cargo between ports in Italy and France. Steamboat technology was still new. Most steamboats navigated on rivers or as ferries, but daring inventors and engineers had recently begun launching their crafts in the seas. Excited by Reveley's plans, Shelley invested two hundred pounds in the project, which was to fail.

The Shelleys rented a cottage in the pretty town of Bagni di Lucca, sixty miles north of Livorno. Casa Bertini, as the house was called, stood high on a hill amid fragrant chestnut trees. The area's hot springs attracted tourists, but Mary, Percy, and Claire avoided the places that drew the biggest crowds. They hired horses and rode into the Apennine Mountains, and they took long hikes in the woods. "I like nothing so much as to be surrounded by the foliage of trees only peeping now and then through the leafy screen on the scene about me," Mary told Maria Gisborne. She wished she had the mind of a poet so she could describe the natural setting in the stirring words that it deserved.

She was glad to be in Italy, but Percy was homesick, especially when letters came from England. Some were from Thomas Peacock, who informed the Shelleys that everyone there was talking about *Frankenstein.* "I went to the races. I met on the course a great number of my old acquaintance," Peacock wrote. "I was asked a multitude of questions concerning *Frankenstein* and its author. It seems to be universally known and read."

The Shelleys had no idea that while they were settling in Italy, several British journals had reviewed the new novel. Most literary critics seemed to be scratching their heads, trying to make sense of this bold book. *La Belle Assemblée,* a fashionable magazine, predicted that due to its "originality, excellence of language, and peculiar interest," *Frankenstein* was likely to be popular. "Fair readers"—meaning ladies—were advised to draw a moral from the story: humans must not play God. For a man to experiment with life and death "must be frightful, vile, and horrible; ending only in discomfort and misery to himself." Reviewing *Frankenstein* for a Scottish journal, the popular novelist Sir Walter Scott drew attention to the excellence of the writing. He remarked, "The work impresses us with a high idea of the author's original genius and happy power of expression."

There were critics who hated everything about the book, however, such as the one who growled, "What a tissue of horrible and disgusting absurdity this work presents." There were too many passages in *Frankenstein* that "make the flesh creep," he stated. "Our taste and judgment alike revolt at this kind of writing."

One man who bought the book wrote inside it, "This is, perhaps, the foulest toadstool that has yet sprung up from the reeking dunghill of the present times."

What kind of novel had Mary Shelley written?

CHAPTER SIX

"The Journal Book of Misfortunes"

The cold stars shone in mockery, and the bare trees waved their branches above me.

Frankenstein begins in the frozen north. An explorer named Robert Walton is aboard his ship, searching for a passage across the polar region. In this remote, desolate place, Walton and his crew spot a man on a drifting piece of ice. "His limbs were nearly frozen, and his body dreadfully emaciated by fatigue and suffering," Walton recounts. They bring the stranger aboard and offer him warmth and safety. He recovers enough to reveal his name, Victor Frankenstein. In the days that follow, he tells his story to Walton, who writes it down. It is an unearthly tale, like nothing Walton—or anyone—has ever heard.

Victor Frankenstein tells Walton that he grew up in Geneva alongside two younger brothers and his orphaned cousin, Elizabeth, whom he came to love. He enjoyed a close friendship with another youth, Henry Clerval. At college in Germany, Frankenstein planned to study science, but dark, forbidden subjects consumed his interest instead: how in death "the fine form of man was degraded and wasted"; "how the worm inherited the wonders of the eye and brain." Working for many months alone, with body parts snatched from graveyards and autopsy rooms, Victor pursued the secret of life. At last he could claim, "I became myself capable of bestowing animation upon lifeless matter." He had discovered how to bring dead flesh to life. From his putrid materials, Frankenstein constructed a massive, manlike, living creature.

The full title of Mary Shelley's book was *Frankenstein; or, The Modern Prometheus.* The Greek god Prometheus, according to myth, created the first human being. He then stole fire from the heavens and gave it to humanity. The gift of fire can be understood to mean that the human race was endowed with intelligence.

Like Prometheus, Frankenstein produces a thinking, feeling being. He expects to be proud of what he achieves. When his work is done, though, he can only look with shock and horror on the watery yellow eyes and shriveled skin of the gigantic "demoniacal corpse" he has endowed with life. Rather than offer it love and acceptance, Victor rejects his creation and his responsibility for it. The monstrous-looking being flees, and Frankenstein falls into a long illness, having sacrificed his health to his work.

Slowly, under Henry Clerval's care, he gets well. He has managed to put his experiments and their frightful result out of his mind when a letter comes from home, bearing terrible news. William, the youngest Frankenstein brother, has been brutally strangled. Immediately Victor returns to Geneva. His family is inconsolable, and a once-trusted servant, Justine Moritz, is charged with the crime. Victor knows she is innocent; he senses that the true killer

Victor Frankenstein stares in horror at the monster he created in this illustration from the 1831 edition of *Frankenstein.*

T. Holst, del.

W. Chevalier, sculp.

FRANKENSTEIN

"By the glimmer of the half-extinguished
light, I saw the dull, yellow eye of the
creature open: it breathed hard, and a
convulsive motion agitated its limbs,
* * * I rushed out of the room.".

Page 43.

London, Published by H. Colburn and R. Bentley, 1831.

must be the brute he created. Yet he says nothing, knowing he would never be believed. He stays silent even while Justine is tried, found guilty, and hanged.

Filled with grief, Victor concludes that the deaths of William and Justine are his fault. To ease his soul, he goes alone into the mountains, to Chamonix. Venturing onto a glacier, he encounters his monster. The creature admits to killing William but begs to be heard and understood.

Listening, Victor hears of a being who began his unnatural life with a giving heart and intelligent brain. Unseen, the creature performed kind acts for a country family. By watching the family and listening as they spoke, he learned to read and speak. Yet his grotesque form frightened them when he approached. "Every where I see bliss, from which I alone am irrevocably excluded," the monster says. "I was benevolent and good; misery has made me a fiend." Killing William was a way to lash out, to strike back at his creator, whom he blames for all his pain.

The monster offers Frankenstein a deal. "Make me happy, and I shall again be virtuous." The thing that would bring him joy, he explains, is for Frankenstein to create a female companion for him. With a wife, he would go away to the jungles of South America and never set foot in Europe again. Frankenstein hates the thought of building a second hideous creature, and at first he resists. Then, recalling the monster's ability to commit evil, he consents to do it.

When he made his first monster, Victor focused on the scientific challenge he faced. This time he thinks only about the possible result: suppose the two creatures produced offspring? "A race of devils would be propagated upon the earth," Frankenstein fears. When the female creature is nearly complete, he can no longer force himself to go on, and he tears it to pieces. The monster, who has been watching him, is enraged. He vows revenge and warns that he will be present on Frankenstein's wedding night.

The monster keeps his ghoulish pledge, and it is Victor who becomes the pursuer. The once-promising student is now a driven man, obsessed with following his monster to far-flung parts of the world—into the forbidding Arctic, if necessary—in the hope of seeing him destroyed.

The novel succeeded because it was "a source of powerful and profound emotion," Percy Shelley believed. "There is perhaps no reader," he stated, "who will not feel a responsive string touched in his inmost soul." Shelley also found a moral truth in *Frankenstein:* "Treat a person ill, and he will become wicked."

Shelley had not always treated others well, but he had been kind to Claire. When August came and it was time for Claire to visit Allegra in Venice, he went along with her and paid the expenses. Venice, in northeastern Italy, was two hundred miles away. The trip would be long and costly, but Shelley believed he was doing the right thing for Claire and Allegra.

Claire and Shelley left early on the hot morning of Monday, August 17. Six days later, they were in Venice, the city of canals. They went at once to the Hoppners' home, where Claire was reunited with her child. Allegra was pale and lacked her usual spirit, but she seemed not to be ill. Shelley went alone to call on Byron, who was happy to see him. Byron was in a giving mood. He offered Shelley, Mary, Claire, and their children the use of a villa in the town of Este, not far away. Byron had rented the villa to use during the warm months but had remained in Venice instead. Shelley and the others were all welcome to stay there, Byron said. What unexpected luck! Claire would spend weeks with Allegra instead of hours or days.

According to myth, Zeus punished Prometheus for stealing fire by chaining him to a rock and having an eagle eat his liver. The liver regrew at night, and the eagle returned each day to feast on it again.

Wasting no time, Shelley sent Mary a letter and fifty pounds to pay for her travel. "Pray come instantly to Este, where I shall be waiting with Claire & Elise in the utmost anxiety for your arrival," he wrote. He threw in some coaxing verses:

> *O Mary dear, that you were here!*
> *With your brown eyes bright and clear . . .*

It took a few days for the letter to reach Bagni di Lucca, where Mary had little patience for poetry. She was too worried about Clara. The little girl had lost her appetite and was running a fever. Still, Mary chose to make the difficult trip. She spent August 30, her twenty-first birthday, hurriedly packing and arranging travel for herself, her children, Milly Shields, and an Italian servant, a man named Paolo Foggi.

Villa Capuccini, in Este, was a bright, airy house with a garden of ripening fruit. Beyond stood the Euganean Hills, where farmers raised olives and grapes. An ivy-covered trellis shaded a stone path that led from the villa to a smaller summerhouse, where Shelley did his writing. He had begun a long poem based on the story of Prometheus, the myth that Mary had called to mind in *Frankenstein*.

Mary arrived in Este too distracted to take pleasure in the beautiful setting. Clara now had diarrhea, and Mary worried about dysentery. This severe intestinal illness has several causes, but in nineteenth-century Europe, contaminated water was the most common one. At the time, there was no reliable treatment; many young children with dysentery grew dehydrated and died.

Shelley thought something as simple as teething might have been making Clara sick. He and Mary watched over their daughter for the next couple of weeks, but they saw no improvement. There was little a doctor could do in Clara's case, but Mary and Shelley decided to consult one anyway. Byron told them that his own physician in Venice, Dr. Aglietti, was the best.

They left for Venice on September 24, hours before the sun was up, to avoid traveling during the hottest part of the day. Nonetheless, the journey was hard on one-year-old Clara, who grew weaker before her parents' eyes and began to have seizures. Shock and dread filled Mary's being. She became acutely aware of everything around her. Every detail of the passing scene, every palace and every tree, imprinted itself on her memory. Years later she would be able to close her eyes and see them all.

After what felt like forever, they were in Venice. Mary waited with Clara at an inn while Percy took off in a gondola to fetch the doctor. But Dr. Aglietti was out, so Shelley came back alone. "I found Mary in the hall of the Inn in the most dreadful distress," he informed Claire. "Worse symptoms had appeared. Another physician had arrived. He told me there was no hope." An hour later, Clara's seizures stopped. She died quietly in Mary's arms. "This unexpected stroke reduced Mary to a kind of despair," Shelley wrote. Clara was buried on a deserted beach in an unmarked grave.

Young children were more likely to die in the nineteenth century than they are today. Of every thousand babies born in Europe and North America, roughly two hundred died before their first birthday. In England and Wales, as many as fifteen of every hundred

Percy hired a gondola, or narrow rowboat, and vanished in the traffic on Venice's busy canals. He went to fetch a doctor while Mary waited in an inn with their dangerously ill daughter.

children age five and younger died. They lost their lives most often to diarrhea, respiratory infections, other diseases, and accidents. But knowing that so many children died did not make the loss of a beloved daughter or son any easier for parents to bear.

"This is the Journal book of misfortunes," Mary wrote in her diary. In it she had recorded the suicides of Fanny and Harriet; the death of her first daughter, the one born prematurely; and now the loss of the second one. She mourned Clara profoundly, but she wept inwardly, deep in a secret part of herself, while putting on a brave, stoic face for the world to see. Her family understood Mary's tendency to hide her feelings. When William Godwin reminded her that only the timid "sink long under a calamity of this nature," Mary understood. She willed herself to go on.

Percy's sorrow emerged in his poetry. In one poem he described a mariner sailing on a sea called Misery,

> *Day and night, and night and day,*
> *Drifting on his dreary way,*
> *With the solid darkness black*
> *Closing round his vessel's track . . .*

Knowing it would help Mary to have something to do, Byron asked her to copy some of his poems. This was a necessary task at a time when writers did all their work with pen and paper. A newly finished poem or story could be full of lines that had been crossed out and words that had been squeezed between others. The author needed a neatly written "fair copy" to send to a publisher. Mary gratefully took on the task.

November came, and it was time to leave Este. The family at Villa Capuccini said goodbye to Allegra, who was returned to

Byron's care, and headed south. Three servants—Elise Duvillard, Milly Shields, and Paolo Foggi—went with them. The group traveled toward Rome and stopped to see the famous sights along the way. They visited the great library at Ferrara, home to rare books and medieval manuscripts. At Terni, Mary again thrilled to the power of moving water. The Marmore Waterfalls, cascading in steps down a tree-covered hillside, were "more beautiful than any painting," she noted. "The thunder, the abyss, the spray, the graceful dash of water lost in the mist below" all inspired wonder in her.

The travelers stayed in wretched inns along the road, including one so dirty they dared not take off their clothes and get in bed. In Rome they felt relieved to find a clean, comfortable hotel. The clear Roman sky, so unlike the misty gray of London in November, soothed their bruised souls. Everywhere Mary looked, it seemed that life flourished amid ancient ruins. Livestock grazed among the marble columns of fallen temples. Grass grew around broken statues that had fallen to the ground. Olive and fig trees had sprouted from ledges in the decaying Colosseum, where long-ago gladiators battled before crowds. In the morning, Mary joined the outdoor artists who sketched the famous structure while William ran and played nearby.

A week's rest in Rome left Mary and the others refreshed and ready to move on to Naples, where they would stay through February. Shelley rented a house on a fashionable street. From its tall windows they watched people strolling in the royal gardens and the white sails of boats dotting the blue Gulf of Naples. Shelley organized outings to the theater and opera, boat excursions, and a day trip to Pompeii, the ancient city buried when Mount Vesuvius erupted in AD 79.

In Rome, the ancient world and the nineteenth century coexisted.

Shelley wanted Mary to be happy, but she needed time to mourn Clara's death, and so did he. His fears about his health returned; he complained of aches and fatigue. He spent hours dwelling on gloomy thoughts, and he wrote sad verses:

> *I could lie down like a tired child,*
> *And weep away the life of care*
> *Which I have borne and yet must bear . . .*

We know today how the Shelleys felt, what they did, and even what they sometimes thought and said from written accounts that have survived the passing years. Studying letters, journals, and other documents is how historians delve into the past. Occasionally, though, there are intriguing gaps in the historical record. Perhaps people failed to make note of what happened. It is even possible that they burned letters or tore pages from diaries to cover up something they wished to hide. There is one such missing piece in the story of the Shelleys at Naples. The few facts that are known about this strange occurrence come from official papers.

On February 27, 1819, Percy Shelley registered the birth, two months earlier, of a baby girl named Elena Adelaide Shelley. He listed himself and Mary as her parents, yet none of their letters or diaries from the previous year mentions anything about Mary being pregnant. So whose child was Elena? Some scholars have speculated that she was Claire's daughter, and that Shelley was her father. Claire complained off and on about illness through the summer and fall of 1818; on the date of Elena's birth, December 27, Mary wrote in her journal that Claire was unwell. According to another theory, Elena was Elise Duvillard's baby. Elise recently had hastily married the servant Paolo Foggi and moved with him to Florence. Either theory could be correct, or the truth about baby Elena could lie elsewhere. The puzzle might be solved if more facts ever come to light, but for now, Elena remains a mystery. The record shows that she was placed with foster parents and that she died in Naples in June 1820.

Days after giving up Elena, the Shelleys and Claire returned to Rome. They rented a house on the via del Corso, a street running through the city's historic center, expecting to stay awhile. Mary liked being back in Rome. "It has such an effect on me that my past life before I saw it appears a blank & now I begin to live," she told Marianne Hunt. She suffered bouts of grief, but not as intensely as before. "Evil thoughts will hang about me—but this is only now and then," she wrote. Mary and Claire took drawing classes. They practiced their Italian, and Claire had singing lessons. Percy found a perch in the Baths of Caracalla, the ruins of one of ancient Rome's largest public baths. There, as he wrote, he felt close to the people who had gathered there many centuries before and the gods they worshiped. He was finishing his poem *Prometheus Unbound.*

Mary began a story, "Valerius, the Reanimated Roman," about a senator from ancient Rome who returns to life in the 1700s and sees the imperial city that had been his home lying in ruins. Human greatness fades, Mary Shelley's story implies. In time, nature reclaims it all. The "vast heaps of shattered walls and towers, clothed with ivy and the loveliest weeds, appear more like the natural scenery of a mountain than any thing formed of human hands," she wrote. As Valerius observes, "such is the immortality of Rome."

Nature performed its steady work, and modern Rome bustled around it. One day, Mary and Claire took a carriage ride through the gardens of the Villa Borghese, an oasis of trees and flowers within the busy city, where they spotted a woman they had known long ago. She was Amelia Curran, who used to visit the Godwins with her father when Mary and Claire were growing up. Unmarried and in her forties, Curran had moved to Italy. She was earning her living as a painter, although she showed little talent for art. She painted portraits of the Shelleys and Claire. Mary disliked the one Curran did of her, saying privately, "She has made a great dowdy of me." Mary later gave the painting away. Curran's picture of Claire is the only image of Mary's stepsister known to exist. And her portrait of William, whom she painted holding a rose, is the only known picture of him. Three-year-old William delighted Curran by chatting with her in Italian.

By May, the air was giving hints of the summer heat that was to come. Malaria would soon descend on Rome, as it did every year. Mary and Percy talked about taking their son away to someplace

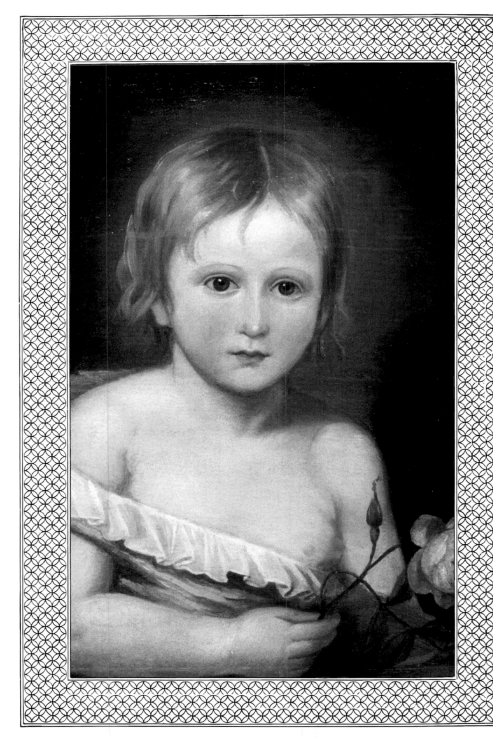

Just one picture of William Shelley is known to exist: the painting by Amelia Curran.

cleaner and cooler. William "is so very delicate," Mary wrote to Maria Gisborne, "and we must take the greatest possible care of him this summer."

But before they could move, William got sick. His fever rose dangerously high, and he passed in and out of consciousness. His frightened parents sat at his bedside. Percy stayed awake for sixty hours at a stretch. "The misery of these hours is beyond calculation. The hopes of my life are bound up in him," Mary wrote to Maria Gisborne. "We do not quite despair, yet we have the least possible reason to hope." A doctor came and went. He was John Bell, a Scotsman who was spending time in Italy. The hoping, watching, and nineteenth-century medical care were no match for malaria, though. On June 7, 1819, William Shelley died. He was buried in Rome's Protestant cemetery.

CHAPTER SEVEN

Sorrow's Abode

My heart was all thine own,—but yet a shell
Closed in its core, which seemed impenetrable...

Clara had died, and now so had William. It was impossible for Mary to hide her sadness any longer. Her despair sank her so low, and lasted so many days, that it frightened Percy and Claire. At times Mary asked herself if life with Shelley had been one terrible mistake. "We have now lived five years together," she wrote in her journal, "and if all the events of the five years were blotted out, I might be happy." She felt a heavy weight of guilt, believing her children might yet be alive if she and Shelley had not taken them to Italy. The thought even crossed Mary's mind that she was being punished for starting the chain of events that led to Harriet's death. Mary was pregnant again, but the stirrings of new life brought her no happiness. She looked forward only to further anguish.

Mary was in such a bad state that Claire gave up her summer visit with Allegra, not daring to leave her stepsister's side. Shelley reached out to Mary, but she had closed her heart to his comfort. In a poem, he asked her why she had gone . . .

> *And left me in this dreary world alone?*
> *Thy form is here indeed—a lovely one—*
> *But* thou *art fled, gone down the dreary road,*
> *That leads to Sorrow's most obscure abode . . .*

He was suffering too. He wrote to Thomas Peacock, "It seems to me as if, hunted by calamity as I have been, that I should never recover any cheerfulness again."

Percy and Mary Shelley each grieved alone. Tragedy formed a rift between them, like a crack in the earth's surface that deepens and widens. Mary also felt cut off from the other important man in her life, her father. Letters came from William Godwin, but his own troubles occupied his mind. He was facing eviction and wanted Mary to send money. She reminded him that she had always thought the bookstore was a bad idea. "How happy we should all be, if you had given it up, & were living without that load of evils!" she wrote. Godwin refused to admit that he had made a mistake, however. "I consider the day on which I entered on this business as one of the fortunate days of my life," he responded. For a while, Percy had letters from Godwin intercepted, to spare Mary that cause of distress.

In her low state of mind, Mary wrote *Mathilda*, a short novel about a young woman's troubled relationship with her father. After Mathilda's mother dies in childbirth, her father leaves her in the care of an aunt while he travels to distant places. He returns sixteen years later for a joyous reunion with his child, and for a time, the two are happy together. Then Mathilda's father draws away from her.

When pressed, he tells Mathilda that she has grown to resemble her mother, whom he adored, and that he now loves his daughter too ardently. Confessing to a "guilty love more unnatural than hate," he commits suicide, leaving Mathilda shattered and unable to recover.

Describing Mathilda's sadness, Mary Shelley might well have been writing about her own: "My heart was bleeding from its death's wound," Mathilda confesses. "Never for one moment . . . did I cease to pray for death. I could be found in no state of mind which I would not willingly have exchanged for nothingness." Mary sent *Mathilda* to her own father, asking him to find it a publisher, but Godwin hated the novella. The emotions Mary had displayed on its pages were "disgusting & detestable," he said. The book's treatment of incest would shock readers, and its ending was simply too sad. He put *Mathilda* away, showing it to no one and refusing to return it.

So the summer of 1819 passed. In September, the melancholy household made its way over the bad roads to Florence, where John Bell, the Scottish doctor, was staying. Mary wanted to be near him when her baby was born. Charles Clairmont, Mary's stepbrother, visited briefly. He had been rambling through Europe on very little money. A young woman named Sophia Stacey also showed up. An orphan raised by one of Shelley's uncles, Sophia was touring Italy with a chaperone named Miss Parry-Jones. This strict, frowning old woman disapproved of the scandalous Shelleys, but Sophia herself was cheerful and friendly.

On November 12, Mary gave birth to a boy whom the Shelleys named Percy. It was Sophia Stacey's idea to give him the middle name Florence, after the city where he was born. "The little boy takes after me, and has a nose that promises to be as large as his grandfather's," Mary informed Maria Gisborne. As she held Percy Florence's tiny form close to her heart, she felt love and an inkling

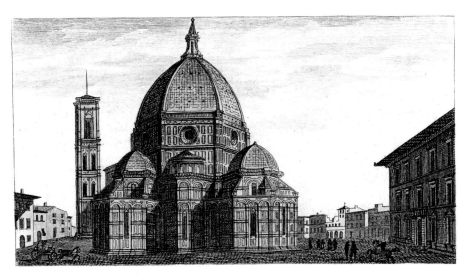
This picture of Florence was drawn in 1822.

of hope. "Poor Mary begins (for the first time) to look a little consoled," Shelley wrote to Leigh Hunt.

Rome had been a monument to the ancient world, but Florence reflected the grandeur of the Renaissance. Paintings and statues by Michelangelo and other great artists filled Florence's galleries. The fifteenth-century brick dome topping the city's cathedral remains the largest in the world even today. That winter, the weather grew bitingly cold. Old people swore that Florence had not been so frigid in seventy years. "Wind! Frost! Snow! How can England be worse?" Mary remarked. Wrapped in a heavy cloak with a gray fur collar, Shelley led Sophia and Claire through Florence's narrow streets to see the sights, with Miss Parry-Jones tagging along. Mary stayed indoors, caring for Percy Florence.

Sophia Stacey remarked on the Shelleys' isolated life. They "see no company and live quite to themselves," she noted in her diary. "He is always reading, and at night has a little table with pen and ink, she the same." Mary, Stacey commented, was "a sweetly pretty woman" whose looks were "very delicate and interesting." Mary wore the high-waisted, puffy-sleeved dresses that were then in fashion. She preferred pastel colors—pink, powder blue, and ivory—and wrapped Italian silk shawls around her shoulders.

Warmer temperatures returned at the end of January, when Sophia Stacey moved on to Rome. Percy Florence was strong enough to travel, so Mary, Shelley, and Claire went to Pisa, the city that would be their home base for the next two years. "We are tired of roving," Mary said. Maybe so, but in Pisa they moved from one dwelling place to another every few months. They rented rooms in one stone house overlooking the Arno River, for example, only until better ones became available.

In Pisa, the Shelleys and Claire found a friend, a woman who had been Mary Wollstonecraft's pupil many years before. Her name was Margaret King when Wollstonecraft knew her, and she had lived an unusual life. When she was very young, her parents had forced her to marry a wealthy nobleman, but at twenty-nine she left her husband and eight children and ran away to Europe. In Pisa, she was using the name Mrs. Margaret Mason. She was living with an Irishman named George Tighe, with whom she had two daughters.

Mrs. Mason stood six feet tall. She had strong opinions, but she expressed them with charm and good humor. She and Tighe often got together with the Shelleys and Claire for evenings of spirited talk, much like those Mary remembered from Byron's villa on Lake Geneva. They discussed politics in England and Ireland, what it meant to be an atheist or skeptic, and the amazing power of the human nose. George "Tatty" Tighe had a vast knowledge of soil chemistry, which fascinated Shelley. The poet made detailed notes on the subject in one of his notebooks.

Mary Shelley wears a shawl in this portrait that was painted after her death.

Both Mary and Claire grew fond of the couple's daughters, Laurette, age ten, and Nerina, who was four. Mary wrote a story for Laurette titled *Maurice, or the Fisher's Cot*. It told of an orphaned boy who finds a home with a kindly old fisherman in Torquay, the

The Shelleys moved from one set of rooms to another in Pisa. The city's famous Leaning Tower can be seen to the left, behind the trees and bushes.

English seaside town that the Shelleys visited in 1815. Maurice stays on in their little cot, or cottage, after the fisherman dies, until he meets a wanderer searching for his son, who was stolen as a small child. Listening to the traveler's tale, Maurice realizes that he is the man's long-lost boy. Years later, Maurice returns to Torquay. The fisherman's cot has been washed away, but he recalls how in that place "he had first discovered that he belonged to good, kind parents; with whom he now lived in content and happiness."

Margaret Mason helped Claire find a position in Florence. Claire was to live with an Italian doctor and his wife, teaching English to the couple's children in exchange for her board. It would be good for Claire to get away from the Shelleys, thought Mason, who saw too much bickering between Mary and Claire. The two cared for each other, but they sometimes found it hard to live together in peace.

Claire left in October 1820, around the time Percy's cousin

Thomas Medwin arrived on the scene. Medwin was four years older than Percy and had served with the British army in India. This talkative gent quickly got on Mary's nerves. She complained in a letter to Claire, "Be one reading or writing he insists upon every moment interrupting one to read all the fine things he either writes or reads." Percy used an Italian word to describe him. Medwin was a *seccatore*— a bore. "He is Common Place personified," Mary declared. What was more, Medwin had no money. He let the Shelleys feed and shelter him and said nothing about when he planned to leave.

Medwin had a high regard for Percy Shelley's poetry, though. He looked admiringly at his cousin bending over his books. "His hair, still profuse, and curling naturally, was partially interspersed with grey," Medwin noted, "but his appearance was youthful, and his countenance, whether grave or animated, strikingly intellectual." He viewed Mary not as an author in her own right, but as her esteemed husband's helpmate. Mary "partook of his genius, and could appreciate his transcendent talents," Medwin thought.

Margaret Mason, who had once known Mary Wollstonecraft, befriended the Shelleys and Claire.

Some friends of Medwin's came to Pisa in January 1821. Edward and Jane Williams had met in India when Edward was a lieutenant in a British regiment. They lived as man and wife, although they were not legally married. Jane had a husband, an army officer she had married at sixteen, but either she had left him or he had abandoned her. English people like the Williamses who defied society's moral code—who lived together without marriage, for example— often felt freer to be themselves in Europe than they ever could at home. Edward Williams was a tall man with a ruddy face who boasted that he was an expert sailor. Jane Williams was small with thick dark hair and large eyes. She had a talent for managing money and saw to it that her household managed comfortably on a small income. The couple had a son, also named Edward, who was almost a year old. On March 16, Mary helped Jane give birth to their second child, a girl named Rosalind.

Mary watched tenderly over her own little one, who was already speaking Italian by the time he was eighteen months old. Percy Florence was "a fine boy, full of life, and very pretty," she informed Maria Gisborne. She was also writing another novel, *Valperga*, which features a real person from history. Castruccio Castracani was an Italian soldier of fortune who led an attack on Florence in the fourteenth century.

Ever since coming to Italy, Mary had been thinking about how to describe the landscape. In *Valperga*, she painted it vividly in words. The beauty of the country around Este "consists in its exquisite vegetation," she wrote. "Its fields of waving corn, planted with rows of trees to which vines are festooned, form prospects, ever varying in their combinations, that delight and refresh the eye." The autumn wind swept over the flat land of Lombardy, she wrote, "scattering the fallen leaves of the chestnut wood; and the swift clouds,

The son of an army officer, Edward Williams was born in India and educated in England. Once grown, he returned to India to serve as an officer himself.

Born Jane Cleveland and legally married to an officer named Johnson, Jane Williams lived with Edward Williams as his wife.

driven over the boundless plain, gave it the appearance, as their shadows came and went, of a heaving sea of dusky waters."

Word came from Byron. He was going to be traveling with his current mistress, Teresa Guiccioli. Four-year-old Allegra was no longer living with the Hoppners, so he was leaving her in a convent. It was common in Europe for the illegitimate daughters of well-to-do gentlemen to grow up in convents and be educated by nuns. Mary understood that Byron had tried to do what was best for his daughter, although she wished he had kept Allegra close to people she knew and loved. For Claire, the news was devastating. "The putting of Allegra, at her years, into a convent, away from any relations, is to me a serious and deep affliction," Claire wrote to Byron. Not only would the little girl be among strangers, but she would be trained in the Roman Catholic faith, and Claire disapproved. Also, who knew how Allegra's health would be affected? She would be better off with her mother, Claire insisted, and "to be benefited by the kindness and affection of her parents' friends."

Byron coldly dismissed Claire's worries. He claimed that he had always planned to place Allegra in a convent or English boarding school. Whether she was raised Catholic or Protestant made no difference to him. Byron would not, however, let Allegra be taught atheism by Percy Shelley. A desperate Claire came up with a scheme to kidnap Allegra. She pleaded with Shelley to help, but he advised patience. "You have no other resource but time and chance and change," he told her.

Over the next several months, Mary made a clean copy of *Valperga* and watched her little one grow. The Shelley and Williams families gathered often for dinner at the end of the day. In November 1821, Byron came to town with Teresa Guiccioli and a menagerie of dogs, monkeys, and exotic birds. Mary liked Byron's twenty-year-old mistress. She was a "nice pretty girl without pretensions, good hearted and amiable," Mary said.

There were excursions to the countryside, where Shelley, Byron, and Edward Williams shot pistols at coins tossed into the air. Shelley and Edward Williams ordered a boat and talked of sailing it that summer along the Italian coast. Mary and Jane Williams listened to their conversation but were not part of it. They said to each other, laughing, "Our husbands decide without asking our consent,

Lord Byron and Teresa Guiccioli savor a relaxing, musical moment.

Edward Trelawny possessed the air of an adventurer.

or having our concurrence." The women were less than pleased with the notion of a boat. "But," Jane said, "speaking would be useless, and only spoil their pleasure."

Someone new showed up. Edward Trelawny was a dark-bearded adventurer who had left England at twelve as a volunteer with the Royal Navy. Having quit the navy after seven years of service, he was making his way through Europe. Mary liked him. "There is an air of extreme good nature which pervades his whole countenance, especially when he smiles, which assures me that his heart is good," she stated. Trelawny held her attention as he told stories about himself, and it hardly mattered that he had made many of them up. He "could not, even to save his life, tell the truth," Byron said. Mary responded, "I am glad to meet with one who, among other valuable qualities, has the rare merit of interesting my imagination." Trelawny described Mary as someone who was "witty, social, and animated in the society of friends." He saw, though, that she could be "mournful in solitude."

Mary wished she could be happier with Percy, but he was spending too much time with his male comrades and ignoring her. He was even paying attention to other women. For a while, he became obsessed with a beautiful Italian teenager named Teresa Emilia Viviani, who was the daughter of the governor of Pisa. Her parents had placed her in a convent school while they finalized details of her arranged marriage. Seeing "Emilia" as a damsel in distress, Shelley toyed with the idea of stealing her away from the convent. He gave her pet birds and dedicated verses to her. He encouraged her to feel sorry for him, telling her that Mary was a cold wife. The infatuation ended when Emilia married and went to live with her husband's family.

Shelley also singled out Jane Williams for attention. He bought her a guitar, and he composed a poem about her playing it. He wrote that in her music he heard

> *The clearest echoes of the hills,*
> *The softest notes of falling rills,*
> *The melodies of birds and bees,*
> *The murmuring of summer seas . . .*

He convinced Jane and Edward Williams that Mary—who was pregnant for the fifth time—cared nothing for him. Observing Mary, who again kept her feelings to herself, the Williamses felt sympathetic toward Percy. His wife, they agreed, ought to have been a more loving companion.

By April 1822, everyone was thinking ahead to the warmer months. Byron and Guiccioli were moving to a seaside home at Livorno, and Trelawny would soon follow. The others planned to stay some forty miles north, on the beautiful bay of Lerici. Once Byron had packed up to leave, Claire came, having been invited to spend the summer with the Shelleys. On April 23, she went to Lerici with Jane and Edward Williams to look for a house large enough to hold them all. While they were away, word reached Pisa that Allegra had died of typhus, an infectious disease spread by lice and other parasites. The Shelleys told Claire nothing when she returned two days later. Percy feared that news of her child's death would drive Claire mad.

They hurried her off to Lerici, to the only house that had been for rent. Villa Magni was big and rundown. It was also isolated. The Shelleys, Claire, and the Williamses all lived together on the one floor that was habitable. Buying food and other supplies required a three-mile trip and a river crossing that was impossible in storms. "Had we been wrecked on an island of the South Seas, we could scarcely have felt ourselves further from civilization and comfort," Mary said.

The others tried to shield Claire from the truth about her daughter, but she sensed that something had happened. One evening she

Villa Magni sat in a lonely, isolated spot.

entered a room where the others were talking and asked flat out if Allegra was dead. The strength and quiet composure she showed after hearing their honest answer surprised everyone, especially Claire herself. "I had a stern tranquillity in me suited to the time," she wrote. "I bid defiance to the dark visitings of misfortune and to the disastrous hauntings of Fate. You cannot inflict more than I will proudly bear." Claire had changed. She was no longer the capricious girl who shrieked when hearing ghost stories. She had matured into a woman who could weather life's cruelest blows. Byron sent her a miniature portrait of Allegra and a lock of her hair. Claire wished to see the body, but Byron was already shipping it to England for burial.

The Shelleys' distress over the little girl's death was more apparent. Percy started sleepwalking and seeing things that were not there. One night he walked out with Edward Williams to view the moonlight reflecting on the bay. Williams recalled what happened: "He complained of being unusually nervous, and stopping short, he grasped me violently by the arm, and stared steadfastly on the white surf that broke upon the beach under our feet." Williams asked Shelley what was wrong; was he in pain? Shelley's only answer was to say, "There it is again—there." He pointed toward something he alone could see: Allegra's body rising from the waves, smiling and clapping.

A strong sense of dread descended on Mary. For no clear reason, she came to see Lerici as a perilous place for her family. She begged Percy to leave. Her pleading became hysterical after May 12, when the new boat was delivered by sea. Mary's behavior proved to Jane and Edward that she was a nag, that Percy's claims about her were true.

When Mary collapsed in pain one day in June, they were sure she was faking. But Mary was having a miscarriage, and she began to bleed uncontrollably. Wasting no time, Shelley sent for a doctor and for ice, but there would be a long wait until help came. Mary drifted toward unconsciousness. "I lay nearly lifeless," she later wrote about the ordeal. The others fed her sips of brandy and rubbed her body with vinegar and cologne to revive her. After seven hours, the ice arrived. Claire and Jane hesitated to apply it without the doctor's advice, but Shelley sprang into action. He filled a tin tub with ice and water, lifted Mary into it, and ordered her to sit still until the hemorrhaging stopped. Shelley's quick thinking saved Mary's life. She was out of danger by the time the doctor showed up.

The boat was twenty-four feet long, narrow, and swift on the water. Byron had named it the *Don Juan*, after a lengthy poem he was writing. The boat's delivery boy, an English teenager named Charles Vivian, stayed on as its crew. Shelley was thrilled. "She is a most beautiful boat, and so far surpasses both mine and Williams's expectations," he said. Shelley and Williams took the *Don Juan* out on the bay. Even Mary, who had seen the boat as a harbinger of bad things to come, felt joy when sailing. She leaned against Shelley's knee, as she had done in the past, breathing the salt air and feeling the sun on her face. Once, after a warm current flowed in on the tail of a storm, they glided on water that shone purple from the floating forms of Portuguese men-of-war.

On July 1, with an experienced captain named Daniel Roberts, and the boy, Charles Vivian, Shelley and Williams set forth on their longest excursion yet. They sailed all the way to Livorno, to see Byron and Trelawny. The Shelleys' friends Leigh and Marianne Hunt and their children were also at Livorno, having just come from England. The *Don Juan* made the trip easily, docking after seven hours. A week later, Shelley and Williams were eager to get

home. They embarked with Charles Vivian at two p.m. on July 8, as clouds gathered over the water. Captain Roberts felt uneasy about the weather and stayed ashore. He climbed to the top of a lighthouse and watched through a telescope until the boat disappeared into far-off mist. Sure enough, within hours, a summer squall blew in. An Italian boatman who sailed into Livorno's harbor to wait it out reported seeing the *Don Juan* struggling against high waves.

Four days later, a letter reached Villa Magni from Leigh Hunt, asking for word of Shelley's safe arrival. This was how Mary and Jane learned that their husbands had set sail on the eighth and should have been home. There was only one way to explain their absence. The *Don Juan* and those aboard it had gone down in the storm.

CHAPTER EIGHT

"And I Live!"

*The ungrateful world did not feel his loss, and the gap it
made seemed to close as quickly over his memory as the
murderous sea above his living frame*

It was midnight when Mary and Jane reached Pisa, having left
their children with Claire. Immediately they went to the palazzo
where Byron, Teresa Guiccioli, and the Hunts were staying. Mary's
appearance shocked her friends—she could tell by the alarmed
expressions on their faces. "I looked more like a ghost than a
woman," Mary knew. Full recovery from her miscarriage and great
loss of blood was still a long way off.

For days there was no sign of the *Don Juan* or its crew. As
Edward Trelawny and others searched the coastline, Mary held
on to a thread of hope: maybe they had taken a different course;
possibly they had docked at another port and were alive and well.
Then, on the evening of July 19, Trelawny brought the news that
no one wanted to hear: three corpses had washed ashore. Two
were easily identified as the bodies of Charles Vivian and Edward

Williams. The third was unrecognizable—too much flesh had been eaten away—but there was a book of poems in its jacket pocket that Trelawny had seen before. The body had to be Shelley's. He was dead at age twenty-nine.

Trelawny spoke to Mary of his admiration for Shelley, and his words helped her through this terrible time. "I have some of his friends about me who worship him," she wrote to William Godwin; she was not "so desolate as you might think." In truth, for the time being, the enormity of Shelley's death had left her numb to sorrow.

Italian laws required that the bodies be disposed of quickly. Taking charge, Trelawny had them covered with quicklime, a caustic substance, and buried in shallow graves on a beach. It was a temporary solution at best; no one felt right about leaving the men in this anonymous resting place. Jane wished for Edward to be buried in England, and Mary wanted Percy laid to rest in Rome's Protestant cemetery, near their son William. So Trelawny came up with an alternative that the women and their friends could accept. He procured an iron rack and had the bodies exhumed for cremation on the beach. The ashes could later be buried where the survivors saw fit. Edward Williams was cremated on August 15, and Percy Shelley on the following day. Trelawny, Byron, and Leigh Hunt were present, but Mary stayed away. "They are now about this fearful office," she wrote to Maria Gisborne while it was taking place, "and I live!"

Shelley's friends had loved him. They saw him as a great poet and felt honored to have known him. It seemed right that the flames from his funeral pyre glowed with supernatural whiteness—even if this was only the effect of setting fire to quicklime. Wanting a relic, as if Shelley had been a saint, Trelawny reached in and broke off a piece of the poet's jawbone, burning his hands in the process. Leigh Hunt seized another piece of bone, which he would keep on his desk

Amelia Curran's portrait of Percy Bysshe Shelley is the
best-known image of the poet.

for the rest of his life. In time the blaze died down, leaving ash and a single organ that somehow had stayed intact. Hunt took it; the friends thought it must be Shelley's heart.

Later, Mary asked Hunt for the heart. As Shelley's wife, she deserved to have it, she said, but Hunt refused to give it up. He was keeping it out of love for his friend. "For this to make way for the claims of any other love," he declared, "I must have great reasons indeed brought me." Like some of Mary's other friends, Hunt believed she had stopped loving her husband.

Lord Byron took Mary's side, but Hunt resented this interference. "He has no right to bestow the heart," he said. After Hunt calmed down, he saw that it was only right to give the organ to Mary. She wrapped it in a piece of silk and some pages of Shelley's poetry and locked it away in the portable writing desk that she took with her when traveling.

Percy was gone; Mary would never see him again. She would never hear his voice or hold him in her arms. As this awareness sank in, Mary regained the ability to feel. She had loved Percy through years of happiness and days of sorrow. Now she regretted every unkind word she had ever said to him and every time she had pushed him away. It was too late to make things right; death was final. She would have to live with the pain of remorse. Because of her stoical nature, she would also do without sympathy from her friends. "Those about me have no idea of what I suffer," she said, "for I talk, aye and smile as usual." No one bothered to notice the blankness in her eyes.

Hunt sent word of Shelley's death to London, where his paper, the *Examiner,* was the first to print an obituary. Other newspapers commented sarcastically on the poet who was renowned more for his atheism than for his verses. "Shelley, the writer of some infidel

Sixty-seven years after it happened, a painter imagined the scene at Percy Shelley's funeral. The poet's friends Trelawny, Hunt, and Byron stand watch over his funeral pyre. Artist Louis Edouard Fournier placed Mary Shelley behind the men, on her knees, although she was not actually present. Observing from a distance are Italian fishermen and their families.

poetry, has been drowned," reported the *Courier*. "*Now* he knows whether there is a God or no."

A letter came from William Godwin, whose thoughts were with his daughter. "My poor girl, what do you mean to do with yourself? You surely do not mean to stay in Italy?" he asked. "Now that you have lost your closest friend, your mind would naturally turn homeward, and to your earliest friend," he wrote, referring to himself. "Surely we might be a great support to each other under the trials to which we are reserved."

Mary's trials were emotional and, like Godwin's, financial. She had two hundred twenty pounds, what was left of Shelley's allowance for the quarter year in which he died. The wrecked boat was salvaged and its contents sold. Sharing the proceeds with Jane Williams, Mary received a little more than fifty pounds. Byron paid her to make fair copies of his poem *Don Juan*. Sir Timothy Shelley sent Mary no money but offered to support Percy Florence—if he was removed from Mary's care. She turned Sir Timothy down without thinking twice. "I should not live ten days separated from him," she said.

She read old letters from Percy, finding both solace and anguish. "My William, Clara, Allegra, are all talked of. They lived then, they breathed this air, and their voices struck on my sense," she reflected. "Their feet trod the earth beside me, and their hands were warm with blood and life when clasped in mine, where are they all?" Shelley, too, was gone, and Mary thought only of his beauty, genius, and generosity. She doubted that she would marry again, saying, "After loving him I could only love an angel like him." Byron seconded Mary's high opinion. Shelley had been "the *best* and least selfish man I ever knew," he said.

People scattered, as if Shelley had been a magnet drawing them together. Jane Williams took her two children to England. Trelawny brought Shelley's ashes to Rome and had them buried in the Protestant cemetery. Byron left Teresa Guiccioli and sailed for Greece. He joined the Greek fight for independence from Turkey's Ottoman Empire. Claire returned to Florence long enough to gather her things. She then moved to Vienna, where her brother Charles was living, to find employment there. Mary and Percy Florence went to Genoa with the Hunts.

What was Mary to do? She was twenty-five years old and had experienced more of life than many people twice her age. She had fallen in love and been married and widowed; she had borne four children and lost three; she had traveled in France, Switzerland, and Italy; and she had published a novel. She had trusted in love, only to have it end bleakly. Yet she held on to hope, because she still had a son who thrived. "I shall live to improve myself, to take care of my child," she vowed. She would also work to make people understand that Percy Bysshe Shelley had been a great poet.

On July 25, 1823, Mary and three-year-old Percy left for England. They stayed with the Godwins in their new London home, a small group of upstairs rooms on the rundown thoroughfare known as the Strand. M. J. Godwin and Company had moved too, and occupied the same building on the street level. Mary reconnected with her half brother, William, who was twenty years old and reporting on Parliament for London's *Morning Chronicle*. She welcomed his company on walks around the city. It amused her to hear him call their father "the old gentleman."

After five years in Italy, Mary saw for herself the great sensation *Frankenstein* had caused. "Lo and behold! I found myself famous," she exclaimed. Her father had arranged for a second printing of the novel, edition that identified "Mary W. Shelley" as its author. One night she went to the theater to see a new play, *Presumption: or, the Fate of Frankenstein*. A popular playwright had adapted her book for the stage. "I was much amused, and it appeared to excite a breathless eagerness in the audience," she noted. Viewers thrilled to see a tall, hulking actor in the role of the creature, his face covered in blue makeup.

Mary earned nothing from this or other staged versions of her tale. She also received no profit from the 1823 publication of *Valperga*, her novel about the fourteenth-century fighting man. This was because she gave the proceeds to her father, who was desperately in need of them. The book sold well, but it never matched *Frankenstein* in popularity.

English actor Thomas Potter Cooke terrified audiences in Britain
and France with his portrayal of Frankenstein's monster.

Helping her father was only right, but Mary had money worries of her own. She heard from Sir Timothy Shelley through his lawyer, and what he said discouraged her. Sir Timothy was advancing her a mere two hundred pounds a year—a hundred for her own expenses, and another hundred for little Percy's. This money was a loan; at the time of Sir Timothy's death, Mary would have to repay it to his estate. Anything that Percy Bysshe Shelley was to inherit would go to his older son, Charles. (Percy's daughter with Harriet, Ianthe, was his oldest child, but wealthy families followed rules of inheritance that favored males. As the older of Percy's two sons, Charles had become his heir.)

In return, Mary had to promise not to take her child out of England. She was not to draw attention to her late husband, either by publishing his poems or by including the Shelley name in her own work. She was not to meet with the Shelley family and was to communicate with them strictly through Sir Timothy's lawyer. These were harsh terms, but Mary had been "the intimate friend of my son in the lifetime of his first wife," Sir Timothy knew. He blamed her for the misfortune of the past several years. He was sure that she had distracted Percy "from his family, and all his first duties in life." Mary's conduct, he thought, "was the very reverse of what it ought to have been." Sir Timothy slept well at night, telling himself he had been more than fair.

To bring in some money, Mary took out her pen and wrote short stories and articles for London magazines. In the essay "On Ghosts," she laments the passing of a world where people believed in fairies, witches, and specters. Much of the earth had been explored, and humanity had entered a wiser age. "Yet," Shelley asks, "is it true that we do not believe in ghosts?" She then tells of two ghostly encounters

Sir Timothy Shelley grudgingly supported his daughter-in-law Mary and grandson Percy Florence. He threatened withdrawal of funds to control Mary's behavior.

that had been described to her. A friend had told of a deceased loved one gliding into his bedchamber and stroking his cheek. Another friend insisted he had seen the mangled soul of a youth whose death had been a violent suicide. Readers were left to ponder whether the supernatural had a place in the modern world after all.

Percy's writings also deserved a place in the world, then and for years to come. Mary wanted readers to love her husband's beautiful poetry as much as she did. She sifted through the pages that remained and assembled a collection of long poems, shorter ones, and unfinished fragments. She published these as a book, *Posthumous Poems of Percy Bysshe Shelley*. She included his "Ode to Naples," in which he compared the soft sound of falling leaves to "light footfalls / Of spirits passing through the streets." She chose the heartbreaking unfinished poem "To William Shelley," in which he insisted that the essence of his son could not be entombed in the earth:

> *. . . if a thing divine*
> *Like thee can die, thy funeral shrine*
> *Is thy mother's grief and mine.*

Shelley had begun the last poem he wrote, "The Triumph of Life," with a dynamic description of sunrise:

Swift as a spirit hastening to his task
Of glory and of good, the Sun sprang forth
Rejoicing in his splendour . . .

In the preface that she wrote, Mary Shelley sought to change the public's mind about her husband. "No man was ever more devoted than he, to the endeavour of making those around him happy; no man ever possessed friends more unfeignedly attached to him," she informed readers. Through his writing, he had pursued the cause that to him was "the most sacred upon earth, the improvement of the moral and physical state of mankind." The proud widow defiantly signed her piece "Mary W. Shelley."

Two months after the book came out, Sir Timothy sent a warning. By releasing this book, Mary had broken the terms of their agreement. He was giving her one more chance, but if she tried again to publicize Percy's writing, he would stop all payments to her. He also demanded that any remaining copies of the book be withdrawn from sale. They were, but three hundred had been sold and would remain in their owners' libraries.

A small number of people had a new opinion of Percy Bysshe Shelley. The moral character of his poetry was "to be judged of from the writings themselves," and not from gossip about his private life, wrote one reviewer. Shelley's lofty images and ardent language taught readers "to rise above petty interests, envy, vanity, and low enjoyments; to investigate and follow out the boundless capabilities of our being."

The editors of one magazine, *The Keepsake*, chose illustrations and then asked authors to write stories matching them. To accompany this picture, Mary Shelley wrote "The Trial of Love," in which a woman's letter to the man she loves falls into the hands of her friend, who misunderstands its meaning.

Other Britons were still dwelling on the whispered stories of Shelley's elopement with Mary Godwin, his desertion of his first wife, and his atheism. In their eyes, Mary Shelley was guilty too. One English lady stated that, years earlier, the women in her family had been "too correct in their conduct" to visit Mary Wollstonecraft, "and the same objection was felt to Mrs. Shelley." Even Maria Gisborne, while visiting London, kept quiet about knowing the Shelleys.

Mary felt lucky to have a small group of open-minded friends like Jane Williams, who accepted her as she was. Mary, Jane, and young William Godwin spent many evenings with a family they had met: a church organist named Vincent Novello, his wife, and their many children. Friends of the Hunts', the Novellos were a musical tribe who liked to gather around the piano and sing.

One of the Novellos' daughters recalled how her parents "made welcome Mrs. Shelley and Mrs. Williams on their return from Italy, two young and beautiful widows, wooing them by gentle degrees into peacefuller and hopefuller mood of mind after their storm of bereavement abroad." The Novellos did this "by quiet meetings for home-music; by calmly cheerful and gradually sprightlier converse; by affectionate familiarity and reception into their own family circle." The daughter remembered Mary Shelley "with her well-shaped, golden-haired head, almost always a little bent and drooping; her marble-white shoulders and arms statuesquely visible in the perfectly plain black velvet dress." (Mary wore black to show that she was in mourning.) This daughter remarked on the flexibility of Mary's hands, and how she amused the children by bending back her fingers until they nearly touched her wrist. The girl treasured her gifts from Mrs. Shelley: a signed copy of *Frankenstein* and a coral necklace from Italy. "Very sweet and very encouraging was Mary Shelley," she later wrote.

Another open-minded friend was the Scottish-born writer Mary Diana Dods. Using the pen name David Lyndsay, Dods had published poetry inspired by ancient myths and Bible stories. It was not uncommon in the early nineteenth century for a woman author to write under a man's name. There were segments of society that thought it improper for a lady to place her name before the public. There were also female writers who wanted the literary world to treat their work as seriously as they would a book written by a man. This was why three sisters—Charlotte, Emily, and Anne Brontë—would use the names Currer, Ellis, and Acton Bell when publishing

The musical Novello family provided evenings of enjoyment to Mary Shelley, Jane Williams, and other friends.

their first book, *Poems,* in 1846. A nonconformist, "Doddy" wore her dark, curly hair cropped short. Instead of puffed sleeves and snug waistlines, she favored plain, tailored jackets. In the nineteenth century, Dods's style of dress was considered masculine.

Through her father, Mary met John Howard Payne, an American songwriter and playwright living in England. Payne had written the hugely popular song "Home, Sweet Home." People throughout Britain and America were singing its comforting words: "Be it ever so humble, there's no place like home." Payne went with Mary and the Godwins to the theater. Because he wrote plays, he often was given free tickets. He was a slim, modest man with thinning brown hair.

Mary considered Payne only a friend, but he was falling in love with her. One day he decided the time had come to declare his feelings. "You are perpetually in my presence," he said to Mary. "If I close my eyes you are still there, and if I cross my arms over them and try to wave you away, still you will not be gone." Mary tried to handle the situation with grace and tact. "Your imagination creates the admired as well as the admiration," she replied. The woman of his dreams was not the true Mary Shelley. This meant his love for her could not be real. Payne's penetrating eyes made Mary think of Percy's, but he lacked Percy's lightning-fast mind and bold vision. He could never measure up to the husband she had lost; no one ever would.

William Godwin also arranged for Mary to see her girlhood friend from Scotland, who was passing through London. Isabella Baxter was now Isabella Booth. After her sister Margaret died, Isabella was pressured by her family to marry Margaret's husband, David Booth. It was an odd arrangement, and one that brought

Playwright and lyricist John Howard Payne nurtured a hope of marrying Mary Shelley.

Isabella no happiness. After years of dealing with money troubles and her husband's ill temper, Isabella had reached the point of mental breakdown. "Be kind to me Mary," she asked.

"The great affection she displays for me endears her to me," Mary wrote to Leigh Hunt in Italy. Mary showed Isabella compassion, but it was impossible to revive the closeness of their teenage years. They were different people now. "All is so changed for me," Mary said.

Through dark winter days and wet spring afternoons, Mary Shelley worked at her writing. She hiked for miles through the city, trying to keep her spirits up. "Ye Gods—how I walk!" she said. One evening's stroll took her past the old, all-but-forgotten St. Pancras

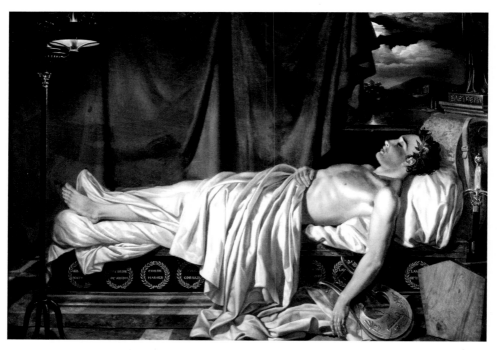

Byron lies on his deathbed in this painting by Joseph Denis Odevaere. Employing artistic license, Odevaere placed a crown of laurel leaves on Byron's head, symbolizing high achievement. Byron's arm falls on a lyre because he was a poet. In ancient Greece, someone often strummed a lyre while poetry was being recited.

churchyard, a place that evoked memories of precious times with Percy. She wrote, as if in a letter to him, "my loved Shelley, now ten years ago, at this season, did we first meet . . . and these were the very scenes."

In mid-May 1824 came news from Greece that Lord Byron had died of malaria at age thirty-six. Mary, already in a low mood, asked, "Why am I doomed to live on seeing all expire before me?" She remembered the good in Byron, recalling him as a friend from happy days on Lake Geneva and as Shelley's close companion. She mourned him as a dazzling figure and a gifted poet. It seemed that Byron's death had left the earth darker than midnight.

Secrets

Permit a heart whose sufferings have been, and are, so many and so bitter, to reap what joy it can from the strong necessity it feels to be sympathized with—to love.

Byron's body was shipped to England for burial. To preserve it for the long voyage from Greece, workers drilled holes in the poet's coffin and placed it in a vat of liquor. Once in London, the body was removed from its whiskey bath and laid out in a private home. For two days in July, the public filed past the open casket. Gazing at the once-famous face now permanently at rest, they saw a mouth twisted open and teeth stained brown by the alcoholic spirits. "Of the crowding visitors the number of ladies was exceedingly great," the press reported. Some distraught fans grew hysterical.

Mary Shelley paid her last respects, but she kept her composure. On July 12, 1824, she and Jane Williams watched from a window as a horse-drawn hearse carried Lord Byron to his family's burial ground in a small churchyard. Mary was living with Percy Florence in Kentish Town, a quiet old neighborhood in northwest London.

William Godwin paces in his bookstore. By summer 1824, the Godwin household in the Strand had broken up. Mary's father had declared bankruptcy and closed his bookshop. He had moved with Mrs. Godwin and young William to smaller, cheaper quarters.

Her home was close to Jane Williams's and near fields where four-year-old Percy could run freely. The two families were close. Percy played with the Williams children, and Jane helped care for him when he had the measles.

Books about Byron were already being written. Percy Shelley's tedious cousin, Thomas Medwin, had rushed to publish *Journal of the Conversations of Lord Byron*, based on his time spent with the famous poet at Pisa. Medwin thought greedily of the money he was to make. Mary disapproved of his project, but she shared her memories of Byron with an Irish writer named Thomas Moore. A friend of Byron's, Moore was putting together a volume of the late poet's journals and letters. Mary helped him on the condition that she remain an anonymous source; she had no wish to anger Sir Timothy. She also refused to take any money in exchange for her help. She cared about spreading the truth rather than profiting from the public's curiosity. Too many worms were growing fat "upon the world's love of tittle tattle," she stated. She would not be counted among them.

Yet a character based on Lord Byron appeared in her next novel, which was published in 1826. Mary Shelley set *The Last Man* far in the future, at the close of the twenty-first century. Instead of a king, the England of that period has an elected leader, the brave, spirited Lord Raymond. Raymond is "supremely handsome," Shelley writes. "Every one admired him; of women he was the idol. He was courteous, honey-tongued—an adept in fascinating arts." Raymond resigns his position to go off and fight in a Greek war for independence, much as Byron did.

Admirers of Byron read a memorial plaque in Hucknall Church, where he is buried.

The world Shelley imagines in *The Last Man* is much like the one she inhabited in the early nineteenth century. Technology has brought little change, which seems odd today. Twenty-first-century readers expect the authors of futuristic novels to imagine the wonders—or terrors—made possible by science. This is because today's readers are used to innovation. New electronic products constantly come on the market; discoveries in fields from medicine to space science are regularly announced. When Shelley wrote *The Last Man*, however, the Industrial Revolution was just a few decades old. Artisans still produced most goods by hand, and farmers labored as their forebears had done for centuries. England's first railroad line was still a few years away. Many people did not yet consider how inventions might alter their culture and surroundings.

Unlike the world of the 1820s, however, the one in Shelley's novel is rapidly headed toward catastrophe. Not only is there war, but a terrible plague is killing off the population. Those infected drop to the ground in convulsions. They soon exhibit the rigid limbs and distorted faces of death, their "stony eyes lost to perception." People die everywhere, and at any time. During a religious service at Westminster Abbey, a singer in the choir falls dead. "He was lifted from his desk, the vaults below were hastily opened—he was consigned with a few muttered prayers to the darksome cavern, abode of thousands who had gone before," Shelley tells her readers. Before long, one person—Raymond's brother-in-law, Lionel Verney—appears to be the sole human being left alive.

In today's novels depicting future devastation, survivors often have a responsibility to pass on their values and knowledge to the generations to come. True to the form, *The Last Man* ends on a note of hope. Lionel Verney gathers some of the world's great books into a boat and sets sail with his dog to search for human companionship.

In Mary Shelley's futuristic novel, *The Last Man*, people could travel rapidly from one place to another by balloon. In every other way, technology remained unchanged. Hot-air balloons had been invented by the early nineteenth century, but they were a novelty that drew crowds of onlookers. This picture is of an 1830 balloon launch in France.

His wish is that "after long endurance I may reap my reward, and again feel my heart beat near the heart of another like to me."

On its title page, *The Last Man* claimed to be by the anonymous author of *Frankenstein*, but readers knew this was Mary Shelley. The book sold well, although many people found it strange and morbid. One critic wrote, "The whole appears to us to be the offspring of a diseased imagination, and of a most polluted taste." Another called it a "monstrous fable" presenting "a sickening repetition of horrors." This reviewer took a jab at Shelley because she was female. "Why not *the last Woman?*" he asked. Everyone knew women chattered too much; Shelley "would have known better how to paint her distress at having nobody left to talk to."

On September 14, 1826, eleven-year-old Charles Shelley died of tuberculosis, leaving Percy Florence as his late father's heir. Sir Timothy Shelley increased the boy's yearly allowance to two hundred fifty pounds, but he could be late in sending it. Even with the three hundred pounds she had earned from publishing *The Last Man*, Mary at times found herself scarily short of money. To pay her rent, she was forced to borrow from Claire, who was working as a governess in Russia, and from Thomas Jefferson Hogg. Shelley's old friend willingly helped her, but he treated her coldly. Puzzled by his attitude, Mary decided that Hogg was becoming eccentric, that he was "more queer stingy and supercilious than ever."

He was also sly. In February 1827, Jane Williams told Mary some startling news: she and Hogg had been carrying on a secret love affair, and Jane was pregnant. The two were moving in together and would live as husband and wife, as Jane and Jefferson Hogg. Jane had been passing herself off as Edward Williams's widow, but she still had a husband somewhere and was not free to marry.

Mary had met a teenage girl who had a secret too. Isabel Robinson belonged to a large family of siblings cared for by their widowed father. She had been involved in an early, brief romance and had given birth to a daughter. Few people knew about baby Adeline, who had been farmed out. Isabel desperately wanted to find a way to keep and raise her child. Mary Shelley understood full well the social, economic, and emotional hardships that single mothers endured. But she also knew the danger of farming babies out. Recalling how deeply Claire had longed to be with her child, and how Allegra had come to a sad end, Mary vowed to help Isabel.

As Claire was discovering, a governess's life could be sad and lonely. She was treated like a servant by her employers, yet she had little in common with the household staff. She worked long hours for low pay.

"Where I see suffering, there I must bring my mite for its relief," she wrote.

Mary began by moving from London to someplace out of the way. She felt no sadness about leaving Kentish Town. "The country about here is really pretty; lawny uplands, wooded parks, green lanes, and gentle hills form agreeable and varying combinations," she observed. "Yet I can attach myself to nothing here." In July 1827, Mary went with Percy Florence, Isabel, and baby Adeline, who had been retrieved from her paid caregiver, to stay in the village of Sompting, on England's southern coast. If Isabel could cross over to France, Mary thought, she could start a new life with her child.

But to do this, she would need more help than Mary alone could give.

It came from Mary's writer friend Doddy. Mary Diana Dods was transitioning to life as a man. She began to wear men's clothing and adopted the name Walter Sholto Douglas. The plan was for Douglas to escort Isabel and Adeline to France; they would travel as a married couple with a baby. In France, they would live on Douglas's small allowance and anything he earned from writing.

Mary sought further aid from John Howard Payne, in London. The playwright and songwriter still hoped for a future with Mrs. Shelley, and she knew that he would do anything for her. She asked Payne to obtain passports for Mr. and Mrs. Douglas. They were too ill to travel to London and do this for themselves, she lied. She asked Payne to have two of his actor friends stand in for the pair. She sent him samples of Isabel's and Douglas's handwriting, so the actors could forge their signatures. No law required British subjects to carry passports while traveling overseas in the 1800s, but the Douglases needed some form of identification. And since photography had yet to be invented, there was no need to worry about passport pictures.

Before sailing for France in October, Isabel revealed some troubling news to Mary Shelley: Jane Williams—now Jane Hogg—had been spreading gossip about her old friend. In London, Jane had told Isabel that Mary had been a callous, unloving wife. Jane implied that Percy Bysshe Shelley had been so unhappy with Mary that he sailed into the storm on purpose, hoping he would die. Mary was taken aback upon hearing these terrible words and hardly knew what to think. She wrote in her journal, "My friend has proved false and treacherous! Miserable discovery. . . . My head weighed down; my limbs sink under me."

Kentish Town offered pleasant rustic scenery, but Mary Shelley
put down no roots there.

No wonder Thomas Jefferson Hogg had been so aloof! Who else had heard these lies? Jane had hurt Mary's feelings—Jane, with whom she had shared so much. Mary had been present at the birth of Jane's daughter; the two women had lost their mates in the same tragic accident; they had helped each other as struggling single mothers. Mary waited several months before saying anything to Jane. At last she confronted her friend in a letter, writing, "You gave ear to every idle tale against me—repeated them—not glossed over them." She concluded, "My devotion to you was too entire." Mary would never be so devoted again, although she felt sympathy for Jane, whose baby had died soon after its birth. The two women remained friends—"the past is too dear to me," Mary said—but not as close as they had been.

After the Douglases left England, Mary enrolled Percy Florence in a boarding school. In mid-April 1828, with Percy settled at Edward Slater's Gentleman's Academy, she went to France to visit Isabel and Douglas. She brought Julia Robinson, Isabel's younger sister, who knew nothing about Douglas's old identity. Rather than sneak away, Mary informed Sir Timothy Shelley's lawyer that she would be gone no more than three weeks while Percy remained in London at school.

Percy Bysshe Shelley's old friend Thomas Jefferson Hogg became romantically involved with Jane Williams. For a time, the two kept their relationship secret, but in early 1827 they began living together as husband and wife.

It was supposed to be a quick jaunt, but upon reaching Paris, where the Douglases were living, Mary felt feverish and achy. She thought a bath might restore her energy, but she emerged from the water even weaker than before. Her fair skin turned red and blotchy, and within days blisters arose on her face and arms. It was plain to all that Mary had smallpox, "the most terrible of all the ministers of death," as one writer described it. This viral illness was greatly feared in the 1800s. It came on suddenly and attacked not only the skin, but also the mouth, throat, and internal organs. It could even afflict the eyes. A fourth of its victims died, and those who survived were left badly scarred and sometimes blind. To prevent the disease from spreading into the community, the Douglas home was placed under quarantine. For two weeks, no one was allowed out and no visitors could come in.

Gradually Mary recovered. One day she mustered enough courage to look in a mirror. The woman who gazed back had crusted sores on her reddened face. The spun-gold hair that used to draw compliments hung dull and limp. French doctors assured Mary that she would have less scarring than some smallpox survivors, but her appearance would be forever changed. Mary made the best of her altered looks; what else could she do? After the quarantine was lifted, she went out to meet Isabel and Douglas's new acquaintances. "It was rather droll to play the part of an ugly person for the first time in my life," she wrote good-naturedly to her old Scottish friend Isabella. She was warmly welcomed in Paris, even by people who knew about her past. At one party, she was introduced to the Marquis de Lafayette, a hero of the American Revolution.

A smallpox sufferer gazes for the first time at his blistered face as two children are ushered out of the sickroom.

As a teenage runaway, Mary Godwin had seen little to like in Paris. As a woman of thirty, Mary Shelley soaked up the warmth of late spring as she sat in gardens beneath chestnut trees newly green after the winter. She drew in big breaths of fragrant air that was so much cleaner than London's. She returned to England in early June and summered at the coast with Percy and Julia Robinson. Nearness to the sea, she believed, would hasten her recovery.

Illness had forced Mary to stay away longer than the promised three weeks, and she was relieved that Sir Timothy was not angry. She was also surprised to learn from his lawyer that during her absence, Sir Timothy had visited Percy Florence at school, bringing his wife and two daughters. Mary was pleased to see the Shelley family taking an interest in her son. She only wished they would give him more money! As she watched Percy at his studies and at play, she could see his character taking shape. He was a typical eight-year-old, sometimes easygoing and at other times quarrelsome; if he insisted on having his way one day, he would give in to his mother's wishes the next; he might be stubbornly silent in the morning but eager to share his thoughts by afternoon.

In summer 1828, Charles Clairmont returned from Europe for a visit. Charles was working as an English tutor in Vienna. He came with his Austrian wife and their two small daughters. Within weeks, Claire arrived on the scene. Her Russian employer had given her a year's leave of absence, and she was spending the time in London. Grief and hard years as a governess had altered Claire. Once impulsive and full of life, she had grown prudish and set in her ways. Watching her dote on Percy Florence and Charles's girls, Edward Trelawny, the dark-haired adventurer, affectionately called her "old Aunt."

Trelawny, who had been such a kind friend after Percy Shelley's death, was back in England too. After burying Shelley's ashes, he had gone to fight in Greece with Byron. He had married a Greek woman, with whom he had a daughter, but by 1828 he was living on his own. For a while he avoided Mary, afraid to see her changed face. Feeling the same fear, Claire steeled herself for "a monster to look at," but was relieved to see Mary appearing healthier and less transformed than she had imagined. She noticed too "the surpassing beauty" of Mary's mind. "Every sentiment of hers is so glowing and beautiful," Claire jotted in her journal.

Mary helped Trelawny, who was writing a book about his early life. Just like the stories he told, *Adventures of a Younger Son* was largely fiction. Trelawny also wanted to see another book written: Percy Shelley's biography. "I always wished you to do this, Mary," he said. If she would not, then maybe he would write it himself. "Will you aid in it?" he asked. "Will you give documents? Will you write anecdotes?"

In truth, Mary had often thought about writing such a book, but Sir Timothy held power over her, and she dared not. "There is nothing I shrink from more fearfully than publicity," she explained. "I have too much of it, and, what is worse, I am forced by my hard situation to meet it in a thousand ways." Unwilling to see things from Mary's point of view, Trelawny accused her of cowardice. He went away disappointed.

When autumn came and Percy returned to school, Mary worked on a book of her own, a novel based on the life of Perkin Warbeck, a real man who lived in the fifteenth century. Warbeck had claimed to be Richard of Shrewsbury, Duke of York. Richard was a child of King Edward IV, who died in 1483. Lacking their father's protection, Richard and his brother were imprisoned in the Tower of London and soon disappeared. What happened to the two young boys is one of the world's great historical mysteries. Many people assumed they were dead, victims of murder, but this was never proved. Warbeck could therefore have been telling the truth, that he was the real Richard and had escaped death, or he may well have been an impostor. In the 1490s, he tried to overthrow King Henry VII and claim the throne of England for himself, but he failed and was executed.

In Mary Shelley's novel, Warbeck is the real lost duke. While researching his life, "I became aware of the romance which his story contains," she explained. "I felt that it would be impossible for any narration, that should be confined to the incorporation of facts related by our old Chroniclers, to do it justice." Shelley used the word "romance" to describe a tale relating the adventures of a hero who displays courage and chivalry as he does his duty.

Perkin Warbeck was paraded through the streets on horseback on his way to imprisonment in the Tower of London.

Mary Shelley gave Perkin Warbeck the finest qualities of her late husband, namely his generosity and love for the good and noble in the human spirit. Both men inspired the people around them to strive to be better. When Warbeck's widow speaks at the close of the novel, readers hear Mary Shelley's voice: "I feel my many weaknesses, and know that some of these form a part of my strength. . . . I am content to be an imperfect creature, so that I never lose the ennobling attribute of my species, the constant endeavour to be more perfect."

Published in 1830, *The Fortunes of Perkin Warbeck* was "full of strange incident and mysterious interest," one reviewer wrote. Not only would it engage readers as a novel, commented another, but "it may impart useful instruction as a history." There was just one problem: too few customers bought the book. Historical novels had been popular fifteen or twenty years before, but the reading public had grown weary of them. *Perkin Warbeck* earned its author less money than she had hoped for and counted on.

In 1831, a new edition of *Frankenstein* appeared in bookshops. It contained a long introduction by the author in which she reflected on her early life. She wrote about her literary parents, her childhood imaginings, and her time in Scotland. Without mentioning Percy Bysshe Shelley by name, she described the summer of 1816, which she spent with him on Lake Geneva in the company of Lord Byron. Hoping to appear acceptable to conventional readers, she made it sound as though she was already married at that time. She also detailed how her most famous novel came to be written. "And now, once again, I bid my hideous progeny go forth and prosper," she wrote. "I have an affection for it, for it was the offspring of happy days, when death and grief were but words."

CHAPTER TEN

𝔐emory

Peace! was I ever at peace?
Was this unquiet heart ever still...?

How quickly children grow! By spring 1833, Percy Florence was thirteen years old and enrolled at Harrow, an old, esteemed boys' school in northwest London. Mary rented a house nearby so he could live at home and save the cost of a dormitory room. His grandfather had raised Percy's allowance again, to three hundred pounds, but tuition and bills for his clothing and supplies ate up half that amount. Even so, Mary paid for Percy to have dancing lessons. Knowing how to dance would help a young man succeed socially, and Mary wanted him to have every opportunity.

Percy Florence was an average student who showed no special talents. He was a chubby, blue-eyed, rosy-faced boy who meant everything to his mother. "My heart & soul are bound up in Percy," Mary wrote in her journal. Percy loved boating, which caused her hours of worry.

Boys play cricket on the grounds of Harrow, the school Mary Shelley chose for her son. Lord Byron had also been a student there.

So much can happen in a mere couple of years. In September 1832, Mary's half brother, William Godwin, Jr., died of cholera. This deadly contagious disease had traveled through London's water supply to infect people in crowded parts of the city. William was active and healthy on a Tuesday, but he awakened Wednesday feeling ill. He rapidly worsened, and by Friday his consciousness was fading. He died on Saturday morning and was buried on Sunday afternoon.

"He was a being of the warmest affections and the most entire generosity of temper," reflected his devastated father, William Godwin, Sr. "All his chosen associates felt a very earnest attachment to him, and a strong sense of his extraordinary gifts." Mary commented simply in her journal, "This is a sad blow to us all."

Word came from France that Walter Sholto Douglas had died as well. Isabel Robinson then proved herself to be one of the world's clever survivors. Claiming to be the widow of a military man, she married an older English minister who had retired to Italy. She and young Adeline went to live with him in his villa.

The Hunts, the Shelleys' friends from their Marlow days, were back in England and had fallen on hard times. With high hopes, Leigh Hunt had launched a new magazine, only to see it fail. Marianne Hunt was drinking heavily and asking friends for handouts, without her husband's knowledge. The two had grown apart. "Lengthening years only made them, in the longer portion of their faithful and unsevered union, strangers," said their oldest son.

Restless and needing new adventures, Edward Trelawny sailed for America in January 1833. He claimed he would never be back, but Mary expected to see him again. She predicted—correctly—that he would return in a few years "with a whole life of new experiences—the tale of a thousand loves." He would be the same as ever, full of tall stories, "yet ever new."

As always, Mary worked hard at her writing. She earned a small, steady income composing brief biographies of important writers for a series of reference books. The publisher planned volumes on eminent men of Italy, France, Spain, and Portugal, but Mary Shelley made sure they included noteworthy women, too. She wrote, for example:

> *It would be giving a very faint idea of the state of Italian literature, or even of the lives led by the learned men of those times, if all mention were omitted of the women who distinguished themselves in literature. No slur was cast by the Italians on feminine accomplishments.*

After listing some of those women, she presented the life of poet Vittoria Colonna (1492–1547). In the volume on French authors, she profiled the politically active Madame Roland (1754–1793), who authored her memoir in prison while awaiting death on the guillotine, and Madame de Staël (1766–1817), a literary critic and bestselling novelist who fled France at the time of the Revolution.

Mary Shelley also wrote a novel, *Lodore*, set neither in the future nor in the past, but in her own time. In *Lodore*, Shelley looks at relations between parents and children. She pays special attention to the education of girls, especially one character, Ethel Fitzhenry. Ethel is the daughter of an English gentleman, Lord Lodore. Hoping to guard her from the corrupting influence of society, Lodore brings Ethel to America and raises her in the Illinois wilderness. There, he thinks, he can preserve her innocence. Like too many girls of her time, however, Ethel is "taught to know herself dependent." As a result, she "seldom thought, and never acted, for herself." In time, the outside world intrudes, in the form of an artist who takes a romantic interest in Ethel. Mistrusting this suitor, Lodore whisks his daughter away. But in New York, as they are about to sail for England, Lord Lodore dies.

In England, Ethel will find love and make a happy marriage, but she will also receive guidance from independent-minded women. How much different the world would be, Shelley suggests in *Lodore*, if women and men were allowed to be equal. Patience would put an end to gossip and slander, and mistakes would be made right through kindness. Rash emotions would be kept in check through a true understanding of right and wrong, "a love of truth in ourselves, and a sincere sympathy with our fellow-creatures."

Mary Shelley labored long hours writing *Lodore*. When the printer lost thirty-six pages of her manuscript, she worked furiously

This scene is of a pioneer settlement in Missouri, but life in the newly settled Illinois country, the setting for *Lodore*, was just as rustic in 1820.

to rewrite them. She pushed herself so hard that her nerves were on edge and her health broke down. Desperate for help, she sent word to Jane Hogg: "Come—My only Friend Come—to the deserted one—I am too ill to write more." Jane had betrayed her, but Mary knew this old companion could be counted on when someone was in need. Sure enough, Jane came with her new little daughter, Prudentia. She stayed for several weeks as Mary regained her strength and good spirits.

Lodore garnered praise for its author. Mary Shelley was "one of the most original of our modern writers," a reviewer wrote. Another called *Lodore* "one of the best novels it has been of late years our fortune to read." The book sold well, but it earned Mary just a hundred and fifty pounds.

At least, her father had found financial relief. Some men who had known William Godwin fifty years before, when they were all young and starting out in life, had since been elected to Parliament. Seeing the well-known author in such dire straits, they kindly arranged for him to get a government job. As "Office Keeper and Yeoman Usher of the Receipt of the Exchequer," Godwin had few duties to perform. In exchange, he received a small salary and a place to live. Godwin, the writer who had famously spoken out against government, now had no problem accepting public funds. All wealth was meant to be shared, he had said, including Britain's. Wasn't he only getting his portion?

In March 1836, when he was eighty years old, Godwin started jotting down changes in his health. His digestion was giving him trouble, and he had a chronic cough. Before long, he took to his bed with a respiratory infection that only worsened. As he fought for each breath, Mary Jane Godwin summoned Mary. For several nights, the two women took turns sitting at his bedside as his thoughts drifted to the past. "He knew himself to be dangerously ill—but did not consider his recovery impossible," Mary observed. She and her stepmother were with him on the evening of April 7, when his heart stopped beating.

With no thought for his second wife's feelings, William Godwin had asked to be buried with his first one, Mary Wollstonecraft. This was why, on the day of the funeral, Mary and Percy Florence stood with the other mourners in the St. Pancras churchyard and looked into Wollstonecraft's opened grave. "At the depth of twelve feet her coffin was found uninjured—the cloth still over it—& the plate tarnished but legible," Mary wrote. This was the closest she had been to her mother since her first days of life.

The government informed Mary Jane Godwin that she had to move out of the home it had provided. Needing funds, she sold her late husband's many books, including handwritten manuscripts of his

This nineteenth-century pictorial graph charts the decades of a woman's life. She begins at an early age to be prepared for her roles as wife and mother. Once she has fulfilled these duties, she declines into old age. It was understood that throughout her life's journey, she would look for support and guidance from her father, husband, and other male relatives.

best-known works. The sale brought in two hundred sixty pounds. The prime minister granted her another three hundred pounds, making her able to afford a new place to live. The family employing Claire came to England, which meant that Claire was on hand to help look after her mother, who was close to seventy years old.

William Godwin had left mountains of paper: letters, memoirs, diaries, and more. Among them was his last, unpublished book. Titled *The Genius of Christianity Unveiled*, it was an argument against religious belief. "What is there behind the curtain?" Godwin asked in its pages, imagining a screen separating the known world from the realm of faith. "Probably nothing: neither 'work, nor device, nor knowledge.'" As death approached, Godwin tasked his daughter with finding this book a publisher. "It has been the main object of my life," he said, "to free the human mind from slavery." He implored Mary not to let these pages "be consigned to oblivion."

She never published his book. Perhaps she was a coward, as Edward Trelawny claimed, but Mary thought no good would come from it. Reminding people that Percy Florence's grandfather had held unpopular, radical ideas might only hurt the young man's chances of success. She also chose not to publish her novel *Mathilda,* although her manuscript was among her father's papers too. A book about incestuous love would make its author the subject of gossip, Mary knew, and she had had enough of whispering and public scorn.

Instead she wrote another novel about a father and daughter. The reader meets Elizabeth Raby when she is a six-year-old orphan playing on her mother's grave, just as Mary Shelley had done so many years before. Elizabeth is a beautiful child, "a garden rose, that accident has thrown amidst briers and weeds." A man, Rupert Falkner, has come to the lonely cemetery to kill himself, but Elizabeth's presence prevents him from acting. Learning that the child is alone in the world, Falkner adopts her, and they pursue a wandering life. Elizabeth grows up feeling a saint-like devotion toward her adoptive father, "a sort of rapturous, thrilling adoration." He, meanwhile, feels "a half remorse at the too great pleasure he derived from her society." Elizabeth's loyalty, he thinks, is more than he deserves.

Falkner is a complex character. He is outwardly tranquil but inwardly guilt-ridden, "torn by throes of the most tempestuous and agonizing feelings." It seems that Falkner holds a terrible secret: not long before he encountered Elizabeth, he caused the accidental death of the woman he loved, named Alithea Neville, who had a husband and son. Time and again, remorse draws Falkner toward death, but Elizabeth's steady love keeps him alive. For a long time, Elizabeth knows nothing about Falkner's past. She reaches her teens and, as can happen only in a novel, falls in love with Alithea

Neville's wondrously handsome son. Falkner must stand trial for his role in Alithea's death before the reader can learn whether the young couple will marry, and whether they and Falkner will live happily ever after.

"Energy and highly wrought passion" were Shelley's "most characteristic features" as a writer, commented one reviewer. He also stated that "Mrs. Shelley wields a powerful pen for a female hand." Like many readers of his time, this critic placed women writers in a separate category, inferior to men. *Falkner* was published in 1837 and sold so slowly that Shelley decided to write no more novels. They took too much energy and hard work and brought too little reward.

Her next writing project came as a surprise. In August 1838, Sir Timothy Shelley gave permission for an official edition of his son's work to be produced. Percy Bysshe Shelley was being recognized as an important poet, so trying to suppress his poetry was now futile. In addition, several pirated editions of his poems were being sold, and some of these were filled with sloppy mistakes. Sir Timothy wanted to see his son's writings presented accurately and correctly. The publisher taking on the venture, Edward Moxon, paid Mary Shelley five hundred pounds to edit the collection and write explanatory notes to the poems. Mary possessed her husband's manuscripts and notebooks, and no one knew more about his poetry than she did.

Sir Timothy had drawn the line at a biography. He did not want a book written that delved into the immoral behavior and unpopular opinions linked with his son. But Mary Shelley found a way to write about her late husband's life in the notes that she composed for the poetry collection. She chose incidents carefully, avoiding anything that might cause readers to disapprove. She wrote nothing about

Mary Shelley as she appeared in the later years of her life.

Allegra and Claire, for instance, or about her own relationship with Shelley before their marriage. She also omitted verses that might remind people of Shelley's atheism or of his marriage to Harriet. She presented Shelley in a way that would make Percy Florence proud, and she considered the task a "most sacred duty." She explained, "I endeavour to fulfil it in a manner [Shelley] would himself approve; and hope in this publication to lay the first stone of a monument due to Shelley's genius, his sufferings, and his virtues."

In her notes, she praised Shelley's love of nature. "Mountain and lake and forest were his home," she wrote, recalling how he composed verses at the Baths of Caracalla in Rome, in a boat on Lake Geneva, or under the trees at Marlow. A true Romantic poet, Shelley gave the natural world "a soul and a voice." He did the same for "the most delicate and abstract emotions and thoughts of the mind." She wrote about his generosity toward the poor cottagers at Marlow and how "this minute and active sympathy with his fellow-creatures . . . stamps with reality his pleadings for the human race."

Mary also wrote about Shelley's aims as a poet. "His poems may be divided into two classes," she informed readers, "the purely imaginative, and those which spring from the emotions of his heart." Poems such as *Prometheus Unbound*, which dealt with ancient myths, were the imaginative kind. The second type—the emotional—appealed to feelings common to all people. "Some of these rest on the passion of love; others on grief and despondency; others on the sentiments inspired by natural objects." "Mont Blanc" is one poem written in response to nature's grandness.

The Poetical Works of Percy Bysshe Shelley, in four volumes, appeared in February 1839. Mary hoped its publication would bring her peace of mind, but instead it brought distress. Other people had

Percy Bysshe Shelley finds poetic inspiration at the Baths of Caracalla.

a different idea about how Shelley's poetry should have been presented, and they made their displeasure known. Mrs. Shelley had been wrong, they said, to delete verses that touched on atheism or radical politics. Her approach was "a falsification of Shelley's nature and history," Leigh Hunt's *Examiner* protested. "Poets don't write for the instruction of boarding schools, but because they cannot suppress or belie the impulses which work within them." Another journal asked, "Does Mrs. Shelley believe that such an edition as this will satisfy the admirers of Shelley? . . . Does she suppose that a veil can thus be cast over Shelley's opinions, or that she can thus charm the world into forgetfulness of the strange story of the dreamer's life?" Thomas Jefferson Hogg was irate because Mary had left out verses Percy Shelley had written in praise of Harriet. Edward Trelawny returned the copy Mary gave him, causing her to note with sarcasm, "How very much he must enjoy the opportunity thus afforded him of doing a rude & insolent act."

All this criticism stung. And spending so much time immersed in the happier past had eaten at her heart. Mary could not help thinking of loved ones who had died too young, of Clara, William, Allegra, Byron, Fanny, and, of course, Shelley. "I am torn to pieces by Memory," she wrote in her journal. It seemed to her that "time may flow on—but it only adds to the keenness & vividness with which I view the past."

Later in the year, Edward Moxon released a revised edition of Shelley's poetry with the controversial verses restored. As a result, he was charged with the crime of blasphemy, which in Britain meant insulting "the tenets and beliefs of the Church of England." He stood trial and was found guilty, but he received no punishment. Attitudes were changing; Moxon was the last person to be tried for blasphemy in England, although the law making it an offense was not abolished until 2008.

Mary Shelley, meanwhile, continued in her vagabond ways. Moving house had become her way of life. After Percy Florence entered Trinity College in Cambridge in 1837, she left the neighborhood of Harrow and found residence in a different London home. It was the first of several she would occupy over the next few years. In 1839, the money she earned from editing Percy Bysshe Shelley's poems allowed her to move to a cottage in Putney. With its forests and farms, this section of southwest London looked like a rural village. From her windows, Mary gazed out at hillsides covered with gardens. She took long walks alone through charming parkland but turned away at the acrid Thames, which flowed nearby, noisy with waterborne traffic.

In summer 1840, she went to Europe with Percy Florence and two of his friends. Nearly twenty-one, Percy Florence was eager to visit foreign countries, although his grandfather Shelley had forbidden him from going abroad. Sir Timothy's longtime lawyer had died, and his new one was younger and more open-minded. He had persuaded the old man to pay his grandson's college costs and to be more lenient with him.

The travelers wended their way through France and Germany and into Italy. The young gentlemen were eager to go to Lake Como, where they could divide their time between boating and studying for their autumn exams. The talk of boats made Mary uneasy, especially since Lake Como was known for its squalls, but she had to bear with her fears and let her son live his own life. She often sat beside the lake, conversing with other tourists, embroidering, and writing letters. Some evenings, alone, she perched in her favorite lakeside chair and listened to the water splashing against the shore. "My heart was elevated, purified, subdued," she wrote.

Left to her own thoughts, she imagined that the world was peopled "by myriads of loving spirits; from whom, unawares, we catch impressions, which mould our thoughts to the good." She dared not guess whether "the beloved dead" were part of this company, but she liked to think they were. "They keep far off while we are worldly, evil, selfish; but draw near, imparting the reward of heaven-born joy, when we are animated by noble thoughts, and capable of disinterested actions."

There were moments, however, when a sight as simple as the curtains or washstand in her room at an inn caused "strange and indescribable emotions" to invade her mind. These objects "were all

Lake Como was a popular destination for vacationers who liked boating.

such as had been familiar to me in Italy long, long ago," Mary stated. "Recollections, long forgotten, arose fresh and strong by mere force of association . . . inspiring a mixture of pleasure and pain, almost amounting to agony." There were also times when her head ached with frightening intensity for no apparent reason, when her body trembled and shook, almost as if she were having a seizure.

At summer's end, Percy Florence returned to college and passed his exams. On his twenty-first birthday, Sir Timothy gave him four hundred pounds and promised to present him with the same amount every year. Percy spent two weeks with his half sister Ianthe, his father's daughter with Harriet, at the country home where she lived with her husband. And, invited by his grandparents, Sir Timothy and Lady Shelley, he visited their estate, Field Place.

Percy Florence would inherit the house and property one day, and that day was likely to come soon. Sir Timothy had reached the great age of eighty-seven.

In June 1841, Mary Jane Godwin died. Claire arranged for her to be buried in the St. Pancras churchyard, next to her husband and Mary Wollstonecraft. Mary Jane Godwin's "affection and devotion to Godwin were admirable and remained unalterable from the day of their marriage till his death," Claire said. After getting her mother's affairs in order, Claire went to live in Paris. Mary visited her there in the summer of 1842, after another tour of Germany and Italy with Percy Florence and some young friends. On this trip, Mary went to the Protestant cemetery in Rome and stood beside her husband's grave. The cypress trees that shaded his white marble gravestone had been planted by Edward Trelawny twenty years before. Sadly for Mary, time had erased William's burial site. She searched the cemetery grounds for her little boy's grave, but it was not to be found.

CHAPTER ELEVEN

Happiness

The turf will soon be green on my grave; and the violets will bloom on it. There is my hope and my expectation; yours are in this world; may they be fulfilled.

On April 24, 1844, ninety-year-old Sir Timothy Shelley finally died. Except for some funds set aside for his wife and surviving children, Percy Florence inherited the Shelley estate. It included Field Place, other property, and thousands of pounds, but much of the money was owed to others. Percy and Mary repaid to Lady Shelley the allowances they had received from Sir Timothy, which totaled thirteen thousand pounds. Next, mother and son honored the informal will that Percy Bysshe Shelley had written some twenty-eight years before. In it, he left money to his daughter Ianthe as well as to Claire and several close friends. Not only was Claire asking for what Shelley had promised her, but she also expected—and received—the six thousand pounds that had been intended for Allegra's support. With this large amount of money, Claire would live comfortably for quite some time. Altogether, the bequests came to more than twenty-two thousand pounds. Finally, the post-obit loans had come due. Portions of the estate had to be sold to satisfy creditors.

Field Place and its surrounding farmland remained, but Sir Timothy had made no repairs to the house for many years. He had hated to think that it might be Mary's home one day. He had preferred to see it fall to ruin than to let her be comfortable there. Fixing the rundown place, Mary and Percy Florence knew, would be costly. They settled instead in London, in a home that Percy chose. It was a new house on Chester Square, near Buckingham Palace. Mary thought the place was pretty.

Inheritance brought its own set of problems. Many people were certain that Mary Shelley now possessed great wealth. Acquaintances came forward, asking for donations to their pet charities or help in meeting expenses. Mary was also bothered by blackmailers who threatened to publish old letters of hers unless she paid them large sums. Often the letters were forgeries, but Mary thought it best to keep them out of the public eye. This was the case, for example, when a slick con man calling himself Byron's son claimed to have love letters Mary and Shelley had written to each other in Marlow. Mary bought up these papers and others, annoyed "to have wasted so disgracefully so much of Percy's money."

The most disturbing incident involved Shelley's cousin Thomas Medwin, who was still trying to profit from his acquaintance with famous men. Medwin had written a biography of Shelley that he wanted to publish. His research had led him to old chancery court records, where he found documents relating to the guardianship of Ianthe and Charles. These pages listed Shelley's atheism as a reason for denying him custody of his children. Medwin threatened to

By 1844, Field Place, the Shelley family estate, had fallen into disrepair. This photo is a modern one, taken in 2008.

reveal the ugly court proceedings in his book, for which, he claimed, a publisher had offered him two hundred fifty pounds.

Of course, he said, if Mary gave him this amount, he would hand over his manuscript and forget about bringing it out in print. Mary had done her best to draw attention away from Shelley's views on religion and sordid events from years before. How dare Medwin dust them off and threaten to present them now? She paid him what he demanded, only to learn later that no publishing house had offered to buy his book. In fact, several had turned it down.

Inheritance also brought a change in status. Sir Timothy Shelley had been a baronet, holding a low rank of British nobility. At twenty-four, Percy Florence acquired his grandfather's title along with his estate, which meant that Percy now would be addressed as "Sir." Having graduated from college, Percy showed no interest in a career.

He was the child of two important writers and the grandson of two more, but he wrote no poems or novels. For a while he studied law, but he gave it up. He bought a boat—sailing remained his passion—and he joined the Royal Thames Yacht Club. In a letter to Claire, Mary praised her son as "always cheerful—always occupied," and called him "the dearest darling in the world." He was a pleasant fellow, but she wished he had some ambition. She also hoped he would find a wife.

As luck would have it, an admirer of Percy Bysshe Shelley's poetry, a young widow named Jane St. John, was visiting her sister in Chester Square. One afternoon in 1847, she entered her drawing room to find a surprise visitor waiting to see her. "Who are you—

A cartoonist drew this caricature of Sir Percy Florence Shelley. Mary Shelley's son lived happily as an English gentleman of leisure.

you lovely being?" St. John asked. "I am Mary Shelley," the caller answered, extending her hand. Seated on St. John's sofa was a slim woman who "had the most beautiful deep-set eyes I have ever seen," the widow observed. "They seemed to change in colour when she was animated and keen."

Born in 1820, the illegitimate daughter of a banker, Jane St. John was nearly Percy's age. At twenty-one, she had gained respectability by marrying an older man with wealth and social standing. When he died in 1844, he left her well provided for. "She is in herself the sweetest creature I ever knew—so affectionate—so soft—so gentle," Mary thought. "She looks what she is, all goodness and truth." The two women became friends, and Mary Shelley introduced Jane to her son. Jane shared Percy's love of boating, and before long, she grew to love him as well. Jane was small and round. She had a way of tilting her head to the side like a little bird. Percy Florence lovingly called her Wren or Wrennie. In June 1848, Jane St. John and Percy Florence Shelley were married. The marriage would be a happy one for all concerned, since Sir Percy Florence and Lady Jane included Mary Shelley in all their life plans.

The three moved into Field Place, which Jane's money allowed them to restore. "It is old fashioned and with few rooms," Mary noted, "but it has a homely and comfortable feeling about it—and that makes it very pleasant." She chose Percy Bysshe Shelley's old bedroom as her own and placed in it the things she valued most, including her portable writing desk. From the windows, she looked out on a grove of old cedar trees. She spoke often about her late husband, almost as though he still lived. She liked to speculate about what he would do in any situation, what he would think, and what he would say.

Lady Jane Shelley was photographed late in life.

Mary Shelley felt secure in the love of her son and daughter-in-law, and she was free of money worries at last. In the fall of 1849, the three took a trip to the south of France. Mary's good fortune should have pleased those who cared about her, but it aroused jealousy in one person. Strong resentment caused Claire Clairmont to act irrationally. She made wild accusations that Mary had had a love affair with a much younger man. Out of the blue, she accused

Percy Florence of not feeling devoted to his grandfather William Godwin. Once, on a visit to Field Place, she began shouting and grew hysterical. She gained control of herself only when gentle Jane Shelley threatened to call for a doctor to give Claire a sedative. At that point, Claire stormed out of the house and broke off contact with Mary.

It was just as well. Drama and strife were too much for Mary to handle. Ever since the summer of 1840, when she suffered headaches and tremors, Mary Shelley had never been in perfect health. She had spells of weakness and forgetfulness; she complained of back pain; sometimes she had trouble moving. She consulted doctors, but none could tell her what was wrong. Living at Field Place, she wrote, "I walk very well—but must not use my head—or strange feelings come on." Writing had become too hard. Her last book, about her travels in Europe with Percy Florence and his friends, had been published in 1844.

Pretty soon Jane was ill too. She felt better if she went away from Field Place but grew sick again when she returned. Something about the house was making her unwell and she could not remain there. In 1849, Percy Florence purchased Boscombe Manor, a brick mansion in a sunny spot on England's southern coast. He planned to move there with Jane and his mother, but Mary asked to return to London, to the familiar rooms of Chester Square, so they all went to live there instead.

Mary was getting worse. She tried to talk herself out of being ill, saying that her health problems were in her mind, the result of melancholy thoughts. But the mental pep talks failed to help. A doctor came and went. In Percy Florence's view, this man "did not do her the least good." While she was under his care, her left leg grew numb, and she spent the final weeks of 1850 confined to bed.

In the first days of 1851, Percy and Jane brought in a different doctor, who told Sir Percy that his mother had a good chance of recovery. Percy felt so hopeful that when Mary's old friend Isabella Baxter Booth volunteered to come and nurse her, he replied that no help was needed. "There is no danger now," he wrote. Touched by Isabella's offer and concerned about her welfare, Mary had Percy promise to send her fifty pounds a year for the rest of her life.

The optimism in Chester Square evaporated on January 23. On that day, Mary Shelley had one seizure followed by more and then lapsed into a coma. Percy and Jane called in yet another doctor who said—probably correctly—that something was wrong with Mary's brain. He did what he could, but the woman who had endured notoriety as the lover of Percy Bysshe Shelley, and who had gained literary fame as the author of *Frankenstein,* never regained consciousness. On the evening of February 1, with her son and daughter-in-law at her bedside, "her sweet gentle spirit passed away without even a sigh," Jane Shelley wrote. According to the death certificate, she died of "Disease of the brain Supposed Tumour in left hemisphere of long standing." Mary Wollstonecraft Shelley was fifty-three.

She had asked to be buried with her parents in the St. Pancras churchyard, but Jane Shelley could not bring herself to honor this request. "It would have broken my heart to let her loveliness wither in such a dreadful place," she explained. Construction of a railroad line had torn up the country around Somers Town, and the grave-yard had been badly neglected. Instead Mary was buried in a cemetery near Boscombe Manor, where Percy and Jane planned to live after they sold Field Place and the house in Chester Square. They had the remains of Mary Wollstonecraft and William Godwin exhumed and placed in the earth next to their daughter. They left

Mary Jane Godwin to rest alone in the old St. Pancras churchyard, which angered Claire.

Claire Clairmont moved to Italy in 1859 and converted to the Roman Catholic faith. She sometimes spoke to writers who were curious to hear her recollections of Percy Bysshe and Mary Shelley and Lord Byron. One who met her in 1873, the year she turned seventy-five, described her as "a slender and pallid old lady, with thinned hair which had once been dark, and with dark and still expressive eyes." He observed that "her face was such as one could easily suppose to have been handsome and charming in youth." Claire died in 1879, at eighty.

Percy Florence and Jane commissioned a sculptor named Henry Weekes to create a statue of Mary Shelley cradling her drowned husband, a scene based on imagination rather than life. It was placed in Christchurch Priory, one of England's largest and most historic churches. Sir Percy and Lady Jane had begun the work that would keep them busy for the rest of their lives: furthering interest in the writings of Mary and Percy Bysshe Shelley and presenting a cleaned-up version of their story. They destroyed many letters and journal entries that cast the two writers in a bad light. When Jane edited a collection of Mary Shelley's letters, she omitted some portions that might cause readers to disapprove. Jane also created a shrine in an alcove off her bedroom. Under a ceiling painted with stars, she placed manuscripts of Percy Bysshe Shelley's poetry, bracelets woven from Mary Shelley's hair, portraits of the two writers, a miniature version of Henry Weekes's statue, and other precious items.

Sir Percy Florence Shelley continued to love boating. As time went on, he dabbled in photography (a new technology) and took up bicycling. He and Jane had a theater built in Boscombe Manor, where they presented—and even acted in—plays. They adopted a

Artist George J. Stodart created this engraving of Henry Weekes's statue. Weekes had sculpted an imaginary scene of Mary Shelley embracing her husband's body.

child, Bessy Florence, who was an orphaned niece of Jane's. Among their many friends was a woman named Adeline Drummond Wolff. She was baby Adeline, the daughter of Isabel Robinson, all grown up. Neither the Shelleys nor Wolff ever knew about the curious connection they shared.

It has been said that when Sir Percy Florence Shelley died, in 1889, he was buried with the ashes of his father's heart.

Epilogue

O listen while I sing to thee;
My song is meant for thee alone . . .

In 1851, the *Eclectic Magazine* printed news of the death of Mrs. Shelley, "the daughter of Godwin and Mary Wollstonecraft." The notice continued, "It is not, however, as the authoress even of 'Frankenstein,' that she derives her most enduring and endearing title to our affectionate remembrance, but as the faithful and devoted wife of Percy Bysshe Shelley."

For many years after her death, Mary Wollstonecraft Shelley was remembered in much the same way, first as the illustrious poet's wife and afterward as the author of one book, *Frankenstein*. Most people overlooked the fact that Mary Shelley had written six other novels, as well as short stories, essays, brief biographies, and even some poems. Anyone who commented on her later work dismissed it as inferior to her one important novel.

That view began to change in the middle decades of the twentieth century as people took a new look at the achievements of women in many fields, including writing. Mary Shelley's lesser-known books had been hard to find for many years, but new editions appeared. Scholars collected her shorter works and brought them out in print. *Mathilda,* the novel that both William Godwin and Mary Shelley herself thought too controversial, was finally published in 1959. Then, in 1997, a descendant of the Shelleys' friend Margaret Mason discovered *Maurice, or the Fisher's Cot,* the story Shelley wrote for Mason's daughter Laurette. The handwritten book had been forgotten in a box with old letters, pamphlets, and ticket stubs. Mary Shelley's children's story at last was published in 1998.

Readers now discovered a writer with imagination, one whose talent was versatile. Shelley had produced a gothic novel and a futuristic one, historical fiction and stories set in her own time. In her novels, she peered into the dark corners of the human mind and heart. She explored emotions taken to their extremes: grief in *Mathilda,* for example, and guilt in *Falkner.* She bravely took chances, as when she presented the thoughts and feelings of an incest victim in *Mathilda.* Mary Shelley also used her fiction to comment on social issues, such as the education of women in *Lodore.*

Of course, Mary Wollstonecraft Shelley will always be known as the author of *Frankenstein.* Her most famous novel has been reprinted many times and translated into numerous languages. Students read and discuss it in high school and college English classes. *Frankenstein* has been adapted into varied forms, from comic books and graphic novels to pop-up books. Mary Shelley's eerily fascinating story has been presented on stage and radio, and it has been transformed into film. The first motion picture adaptation was created by Thomas Edison in 1910. The most famous Hollywood version, starring Boris Karloff as the creature, opened in theaters in 1931 and is still widely seen. Released in 1974, *Young Frankenstein*, directed by Mel Brooks and starring Gene Wilder, is now a comedy classic.

Thomas Edison was the first person to turn *Frankenstein* into a motion picture, in 1910. Edison's film had a running time of sixteen minutes.

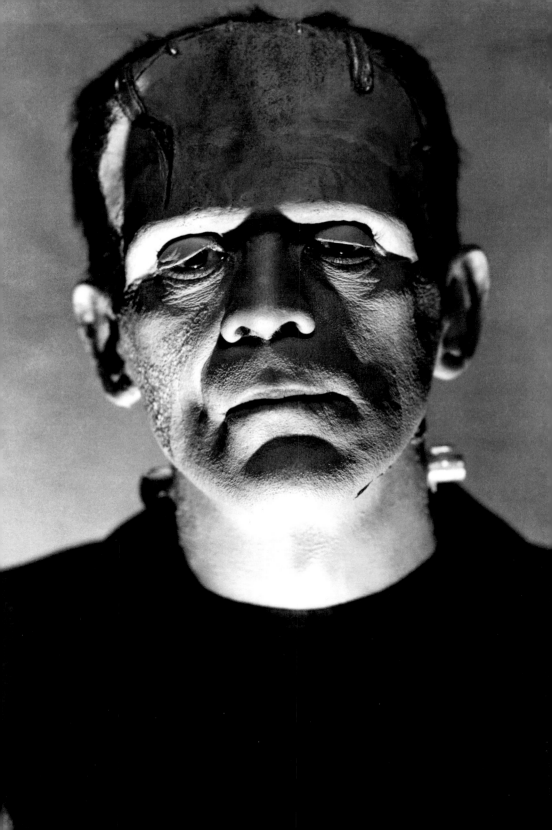

Frankenstein has inspired cartoons, TV shows, songs, video games, and a breakfast cereal. The list of pop-culture references is endless.

But then, who can resist traveling with Mary Shelley to that rainy November night when, by the light of a sputtering candle, Victor Frankenstein first sees "the dull yellow eye of the creature open"?

Boris Karloff's portrayal of the creature in the 1931 film *Frankenstein* is the best-known image of literature's most famous monster.

Notes

Opening verses

ii "Who shall conceive . . ." Mary Wollstonecraft Shelley, *Frankenstein*, 33.

vii "So now my summer-task is ended . . .": Mary Wollstonecraft Shelley, ed., *The Poetical Works of Percy Bysshe Shelley*, vol. 1, 155.

"How like a star . . .": Mary Wollstonecraft Shelley, "Stanzas," 179.

Prologue

1 "If the world . . .": Mary Wollstonecraft Shelley, *Mathilda*, 215.

2 "Every thing must have a beginning . . .": Mary Wollstonecraft Shelley, *Frankenstein*, 167.

"I did not make . . .": Ibid., 166.

CHAPTER ONE

Imagination

3 "The solitary thoughts . . .": Mary Wollstonecraft Shelley, *Falkner*, 69.

5 "the most oppressed . . .": Mary Wollstonecraft, *A Vindication of the Rights of Woman*, 210.

6 "Whenever government assumes . . .": William Godwin, *An Enquiry Concerning Political Justice*, vol. 2, 143.

8 "Be happy . . .": Ralph M. Wardle, *Godwin & Mary*, 17.

"I am the most unfit person . . .": Mrs. Julian Marshall, *The Life and Letters of Mary Wollstonecraft Shelley*, vol. 1, 14.

9 "Is it possible . . .": William St. Clair, *The Godwins and the Shelleys*, 238.

10   "great genius . . .": C. Kegan Paul, *William Godwin: His Friends and Contemporaries,* vol. 2, 5.

11   "ice, mast high . . .": Samuel Taylor Coleridge, *The Rime of the Ancient Mariner,* 21.

"slimy things . . .": Ibid., 31.

"singularly bold . . .": Marshall, *The Life and Letters of Mary Wollstonecraft Shelley,* vol. 1, 35.

"too grave and severe": Kegan Paul, *William Godwin,* vol. 1, 37.

"other objects and avocations . . .": Marshall, *The Life and Letters of Mary Wollstonecraft Shelley,* vol. 1, 28.

12   "Seeds of intellect . . .": Frederick L. Jones, ed., *The Letters of Percy Bysshe Shelley,* vol. 1, 279.

"we may learn . . .": William Scolfield [William Godwin], *Bible Stories,* v.

14   "[dashing] their brains out . . .": Charles Lamb, *The Adventures of Ulysses,* 8.

"a sensible, amiable woman . . .": Mark Van Doren, ed., *Correspondence of Aaron Burr and His Daughter Theodosia,* 264.

"les goddesses": Matthew L. Davis, *The Private Journal of Aaron Burr,* vol. 2, 318.

15   "I do not desire . . .": Marshall, *The Life and Letters of Mary Wollstonecraft Shelley,* vol. 1, 28.

17   "the eyry of freedom . . .": M. W. Shelley, *Frankenstein,* 166.

"At fourteen and fifteen . . .": M. W. Shelley, *Falkner,* 68.

CHAPTER TWO

Escape!

21   "Love is to me . . .": Mary Wollstonecraft Shelley, *The Last Man,* vol. 1, 74.

"I must speak with Godwin . . .": Thomas Jefferson Hogg, *The Life of Percy Bysshe Shelley,* vol. 2, 537.

21 "Bysshe strode about the room . . .": Ibid.

22 "A thrilling voice . . .": Ibid., 538.

"Do you think . . .": Ibid.

"of a sunny and burnished brightness . . .": Marion Kingston Stocking, ed., *The Journals of Claire Clairmont*, 431.

23 "Upon my heart . . .": Thomas Hutchinson, ed., *Shelley: Poetical Works*, 522.

24 "Gain experience . . .": Mary Wollstonecraft, *Maria*, 35.

"at first with the confidence of friendship . . .": *The Bodleian Shelley Manuscripts*, vol. 22, part 2, 266–67.

"The sublime and rapturous moment . . .": Miranda Seymour, *Mary Shelley*, 93.

"I could not believe . . .": St. Clair, *The Godwins and the Shelleys*, 362.

"to give up . . .": Richard Holmes, *Shelley*, 232.

25 "His eyes were bloodshot . . .": H. F. B. Brett-Smith, ed., *Peacock's Memoirs of Shelley*, 47–48.

26 "Our connection . . .": Holmes, *Shelley*, 234.

"looked extremely wild": Edward Dowden, *The Life of Percy Bysshe Shelley*, vol. 2, 544.

"They wish to separate us . . .": Ibid.

"I won't take this laudanum . . .": Ibid.

27 "love, though young and unacknowledged . . .": M. W. Shelley, *Falkner*, 98.

"She was in my arms . . .": Seymour, *Mary Shelley*, 98.

28 "The art of travelling . . .": Mary Wollstonecraft, unsigned book review in the *Analytical Review*, May–August 1790, 375.

"Look, Mary . . .": Holmes, *Shelley*, 235.

30 "the women with high caps . . .": Mary Wollstonecraft Shelley, ed., *Essays, Letters from Abroad, Translations and Fragments*, 80.

"Our own perceptions . . .": Paula R. Feldman and Diana Scott-Kilvert, eds., *The Journals of Mary Shelley, 1814–1844*, vol. 1, 9.

31 "now the houses . . .": M. W. Shelley, ed., *Essays, Letters from Abroad, Translations and Fragments*, 82.

"You will at least . . .": Holmes, *Shelley*, 238.

32 "What was my surprize . . .": Stocking, ed., *The Journals of Claire Clairmont*, 27.

"On every side . . .": M. W. Shelley, ed., *Essays, Letters from Abroad, Translations and Fragments*, 47.

33 "sinks into melancholy . . .": Mary Wollstonecraft, *Letters Written during a Short Residence in Sweden, Norway, and Denmark*, 71.

34 "The Ideot": Seymour, *Mary Shelley*, 112.

"The face of the Captain . . .": Stocking, ed., *The Journals of Claire Clairmont*, 41.

CHAPTER THREE
Life's Lessons

35 "While we are young . . .": M. W. Shelley, *Falkner*, 231.

36 "I detest Mrs G.": Betty T. Bennett, ed., *The Letters of Mary Wollstonecraft Shelley*, vol. 1, 3.

"Dear good creature . . .": Ibid.

37 "He cares not . . .": Jones, ed., *The Letters of Percy Bysshe Shelley*, vol. 1, 421.

38 "witching time of night . . .": Marshall, *The Life and Letters of Mary Wollstonecraft Shelley*, vol. 1, 91.

39 "Mary love . . .": Jones, ed., *The Letters of Percy Bysshe Shelley*, vol. 1, 414.

". . . all my being . . .": M. W. Shelley, ed., *The Poetical Works of Percy Bysshe Shelley*, vol. 4, 71.

"Love in idleness": Marshall, *The Life and Letters of Mary Wollstonecraft Shelley*, vol. 1, 98.

39 "To sleep & talk . . .": Stocking, ed., *The Journals of Claire Clairmont*, 58.

40 "[I] think of my little dead baby . . .": Marshall, *The Life and Letters of Mary Wollstonecraft Shelley*, vol. 1, 110.

41 "How does the meadow-flower . . .": Henry Reed, ed., *The Complete Poetical Works of William Wordsworth*, 233.

"his teeth so many stationary smiles . . .": Karl Elze, *Lord Byron: A Biography*, 332.

"the gentleman with the beautiful voice": Ibid., 333.

42 "To climb the trackless mountain . . .": George Gordon, Lord Byron, *The Complete Works of Lord Byron*, 102.

"Mary's illness disappears . . .": Marshall, *The Life and Letters of Mary Wollstonecraft Shelley*, vol. 1, 99.

"I like him better . . .": Ibid., 102.

44 "veilèd maid . . .": Percy Bysshe Shelley, *The Complete Poetical Works of Percy Bysshe Shelley*, vol. 1, 256.

45 "the worship of the majesty . . .": Ibid., 271.

"Shelley even proposed . . .": Jones, ed., *The Letters of Percy Bysshe Shelley*, vol. 1, 490.

46 "thus harsh and cruel": Marshall, *The Life and Letters of Mary Wollstonecraft Shelley*, vol. 1, 127.

"mad, bad, and dangerous . . .": Frances Wilson, ed., *Byromania*, 200.

47 "about the distance . . .": Rowland E. Prothero, ed., *The Works of Lord Byron*, vol. 3, 436.

"like music on the waters . . .": Byron, *The Complete Works of Lord Byron*, 328.

"Mary is delighted . . .": Marion Kingston Stocking, ed., *The Clairmont Correspondence*, vol. 1, 40.

"Were I to float . . .": Ibid., 44.

CHAPTER FOUR

Year Without a Summer

49   "I busied myself . . .": M. W. Shelley, *Frankenstein*, 167.

     "The lovely lake . . .": M. W. Shelley, ed., *Essays, Letters from Abroad, Translations and Fragments*, 91.

50   "a parcel of staring boobies": Thomas Moore, ed., *Letters and Journals of Lord Byron*, vol. 2, 319.

     "family of very suspicious appearance . . .": Seymour, *Mary Shelley*, 153.

     "social hatred": Jones, ed., *The Letters of Percy Bysshe Shelley*, vol. 2, 329.

51   "like a wild animal . . .": Holmes, *Shelley*, 339.

     "All things that move . . .": *History of a Six Weeks' Tour*, 175–83.

52   "the year without a summer": C. R. Harington, ed., *The Year Without a Summer?*, 6.

54   "I see the animal functions . . .": William Lawrence, *Lectures on Physiology, Zoology, and the Natural History of Man*, 6.

     "We will each write . . .": William Michael Rossetti, ed., *The Diary of Dr. John William Polidori*, 126.

     "with shut eyes . . .": Mary Wollstonecraft Shelley, *Mary Shelley: The Dover Reader*, 9.

56   "a thrill of fear . . .": Ibid.

     "What terrified me . . .": Ibid.

     "But for his incitement . . .": Ibid., 10.

57   "I never loved . . .": Richard Lansdown, ed., *Byron's Letters and Journals*, 261.

59   "I shall ever love thee": Feldman and Scott-Kilvert, eds., *The Journals of Mary Shelley*, vol. 1, 172.

     "I shall love you . . .": Seymour, *Mary Shelley*, 163–64.

     "put an end to the existence . . .": Kegan Paul, *William Godwin*, vol. 2, 242.

60 "My advice and earnest prayer . . .": Dowden, *The Life of Percy Bysshe Shelley*, vol. 2, 58.

61 "my house would then have been a proper asylum . . .": Ibid., 70.

"Mary is reading . . .": Seymour, *Mary Shelley*, 167.

62 "the happiest and *longest* two years": Tomalin, *Shelley and His World*, 62.

"How very happy shall I be . . .": Marshall, *The Life and Letters of Mary Wollstonecraft Shelley*, vol. 1, 177.

63 "You can scarcely imagine . . .": St. Clair, *The Godwins and the Shelleys*, 417.

64 "was safely delivered . . .": John Murray, ed., *Lord Byron's Correspondence*, vol. 2, 31–32.

CHAPTER FIVE

Dreams

65 "While there is life . . .": M. W. Shelley, *The Last Man*, vol. 1, 42.

"a very striking . . .": Dowden, *The Life of Percy Bysshe Shelley*, vol. 2, 60.

67 "liberty-loving . . .": Anthony Holden, *The Wit in the Dungeon*, 104.

"Adonis . . .": "The Prince on St. Patrick's Day," 179.

68 "sedate-faced young lady . . .": Thornton Hunt, ed., *The Correspondence of Leigh Hunt*, vol. 1, 134.

"nymph of the sidelong looks": Ibid., 129.

"in the paleness . . .": M. W. Shelley, ed., *The Poetical Works of Percy Bysshe Shelley*, vol. 1, 155.

69 "is very comfortable . . .": Holmes, *Shelley*, 368.

"the most wonderful work . . .": Marshall, *The Life and Letters of Mary Wollstonecraft Shelley*, vol. 2, p. 69.

70 "little information, no reflection . . .": *Blackwood's Edinburgh Magazine*, July 1818, 412.

74 "Country town friends . . .": Bennett, ed., *The Letters of Mary Wollstonecraft Shelley*, vol. 1, 58.

74　*Le rêve est fini*": Seymour, *Mary Shelley*, 197.

"The little Commodore": Marshall, *The Life and Letters of Mary Wollstonecraft Shelley*, vol. 1, 203.

75　"the fruit trees . . .": Bennett, ed., *The Letters of Mary Wollstonecraft Shelley*, vol. 1, 63–64.

76　"My dear Lord Byron . . .": Seymour, *Mary Shelley*, 206.

"requires reassurance . . .": Holmes, *Shelley*, 419.

77　"They dress her . . .": Bennett, ed., *The Letters of Mary Wollstonecraft Shelley*, vol. 1, 68.

78　"She is reserved . . .": Dowden, *The Life of Percy Bysshe Shelley*, vol. 2, 209.

"How inexpressibly pleasing . . .": Marshall, *The Life and Letters of Mary Wollstonecraft Shelley*, vol. 1, 216.

79　"I like nothing so much . . .": *The Bodleian Shelley Manuscripts*, vol. 5, 364.

"I went to the races . . .": Richard Garnett, ed., *Thomas Love Peacock*, 75.

"originality, excellence of language . . .": Untitled review of *Frankenstein*, in *La Belle Assemblée*, March 1818.

"The work impresses us . . .": "Remarks on *Frankenstein*" in *Blackwoods Edinburgh Magazine*, 620.

"What a tissue . . .": Untitled review of *Frankenstein*, in the *Quarterly Review*, October 1817–May 1818, 382.

80　"make the flesh creep . . .": Ibid., 385.

"This is, perhaps . . .": *The Hamilton Palace Libraries*, 138.

CHAPTER SIX

"The Journal Book of Misfortunes"

81　"The cold stars . . .": M. W. Shelley, *Frankenstein*, 95.

"His limbs were nearly frozen . . .": Ibid., 14.

82　"the fine form . . .": Ibid., 31.

"I became myself capable . . .": Ibid., 47.

82 "demoniacal corpse": Ibid., 53.

84 "Everywhere I see bliss . . .": Ibid., 91.

"A race of devils . . .": Ibid., 119.

85 "a source of powerful and profound emotion . . .": Percy Bysshe Shelley, "On 'Frankenstein'" in *Athenaeum*, 730.

86 "Pray come instantly . . .": Holmes, *Shelley*, 443.

"O Mary dear . . .": M. W. Shelley, ed., *The Poetical Works of Percy Bysshe Shelley*, vol. 3, 143.

88 "I found Mary . . .": Dowden, *The Life of Percy Bysshe Shelley*, vol. 2, 231.

89 "This is the Journal book . . .": Feldman and Scott-Kilvert, eds., *The Journals of Mary Shelley*, vol. 1, 226.

"sink long under a calamity . . .": Seymour, *Mary Shelley*, 215.

"Day and night . . .": M. W. Shelley, ed., *The Poetical Works of Percy Bysshe Shelley*, vol. 3, 127.

90 "more beautiful . . .": Dowden, *The Life of Percy Bysshe Shelley*, vol. 2, 245.

91 "I could lie down . . .": M. W. Shelley, ed., *The Poetical Works of Percy Bysshe Shelley*, vol. 3, 152.

92 "It has such an effect . . .": Bennett, ed., *The Letters of Mary Wollstonecraft Shelley*, vol. 1, 89.

"Evil thoughts will hang about me . . .": Ibid., 91.

93 "vast heaps of shattered walls . . .": Charles E. Robinson, ed., *Mary Shelley: Collected Tales and Stories*, 340.

"such is the immortality . . .": Ibid., 341.

"she has made . . .": E. J. Trelawny, "Shelley's Last Days" in *Athenaeum*, 144.

95 "is so very delicate . . .": Bennett, ed., *The Letters of Mary Wollstonecraft Shelley*, vol. 1, 98.

"The misery of these hours . . .": Dowden, *The Life of Percy Bysshe Shelley*, vol. 2, 267.

CHAPTER SEVEN

Sorrow's Abode

96 "My heart was all thine own . . .": M. W. Shelley, "The Choice," in Harry Buxton Forman, ed., *The Poetical Works of Percy Bysshe Shelley*, vol. 1, 4.

"We have now lived . . .": Marshall, *The Life and Letters of Mary Wollstonecraft Shelley*, vol. 1, 244.

97 "And left me . . .": P. B. Shelley, *The Complete Poetical Works of Percy Bysshe Shelley*, vol. 3, 231.

"It seems to me . . .": Ingpen, ed., *The Letters of Percy Bysshe Shelley*, vol. 2, 692.

"How happy we should all be . . .": Bennett, ed., *The Letters of Mary Wollstonecraft Shelley*, vol. 1, 134.

"I consider the day . . .": Kegan Paul, *William Godwin*, vol. 2, 270.

98 "guilty love . . .": M. W. Shelley, *Mathilda*, 72.

"My heart was bleeding . . .": Ibid., 94.

"disgusting & detestable . . .": Frederick L. Jones, ed., *Maria Gisborne and Edward E. Williams*, 45.

"The little boy . . .": Bennett, ed., *The Letters of Mary Wollstonecraft Shelley*, vol. 1, 112.

99 "Poor Mary begins . . .": Ingpen, ed., *The Letters of Percy Bysshe Shelley*, vol. 2, 747.

"Wind! Frost! Snow . . .": Bennett, ed., *The Letters of Mary Wollstonecraft Shelley*, vol. 1, 124.

"see no company . . .": Helen Rossetti Angeli, *Shelley and His Friends in Italy*, 96–97.

"a sweetly pretty woman . . .": Ibid., 98.

100 "We are tired . . .": Bennett, ed., *The Letters of Mary Wollstonecraft Shelley*, vol. 1, 124.

102 "he had first discovered . . .": Mary Wollstonecraft Shelley, *Maurice, or the Fisher's Cot*, 115.

103 "Be one reading . . .": Seymour, *Mary Shelley*, 256.

103 "He is Common Place . . .": Ibid.

"His hair, still profuse . . .": Thomas Medwin, *The Life of Percy Bysshe Shelley*, vol. 2, 2.

"partook of his genius . . .": Thomas Medwin, *Memoir of Percy Bysshe Shelley*, 57.

104 "a fine boy . . .": Marshall, *The Life and Letters of Mary Wollstonecraft Shelley*, vol. 1, 341.

"consists in its exquisite vegetation . . .": Mary Wollstonecraft Shelley, *Valperga*, vol. 1, 44.

106 "scattering the fallen leaves . . .": Ibid., 45.

"the putting of Allegra . . .": Robert Gittings and Jo Manton, *Claire Clairmont and the Shelleys*, 59.

"You have no other resource . . .": Ingpen, ed., *The Letters of Percy Bysshe Shelley*, vol. 2, 942.

107 "nice pretty girl . . .": Marshall, *The Life and Letters of Mary Wollstonecraft Shelley*, vol. 1, 317.

"Our husbands decide . . .": Dowden, *The Life of Percy Bysshe Shelley*, vol. 2, 465.

108 "There is an air . . .": Marshall, *The Life and Letters of Mary Wollstonecraft Shelley*, vol. 1, 321.

"could not, even to save his life . . .": Julius Millingen, *Memoirs of the Affairs of Greece*, 153.

"I am glad . . .": Marshall, *The Life and Letters of Mary Wollstonecraft Shelley*, vol. 1, 322.

"witty, social, and animated . . .": William Michael Rossetti, "Shelley's Life and Writings" in *Dublin University Magazine*, 146.

109 "The clearest echoes . . .": P. B. Shelley, *The Complete Poetical Works of Percy Bysshe Shelley*, vol. 3, 114.

"Had we been wrecked . . .": Dowden, *The Life of Percy Bysshe Shelley*, vol. 2, 498.

111   "I had a stern tranquillity . . .": Stocking, ed., *The Journals of Claire Clairmont*, 436–37.

"He complained of being . . .": Marshall, *The Life and Letters of Mary Wollstonecraft Shelley*, vol. 1, 349.

112   "I lay nearly lifeless": Bennett, ed., *The Letters of Mary Wollstonecraft Shelley*, vol. 1, 244.

"She is a most beautiful boat . . .": Ingpen, ed., *The Letters of Percy Bysshe Shelley*, vol. 2, 966.

CHAPTER EIGHT

"And I Live!"

115   "The ungrateful world . . .": Mary Wollstonecraft Shelley, ed., *Posthumous Poems of Percy Bysshe Shelley*, iv.

"I looked more like a ghost . . .": Bennett, ed., *The Letters of Mary Wollstonecraft Shelley*, vol. 1, 247.

116   "I have some of his friends . . .": Ibid., vol. 3, 401.

"They are now about this . . .": Marshall, *The Life and Letters of Mary Wollstonecraft Shelley*, vol. 2, 20.

118   "For this to make way . . .": Holden, *The Wit in the Dungeon*, 166.

"Those about me . . .": Bennett, ed., *The Letters of Mary Wollstonecraft Shelley*, vol. 1, 261.

119   "Shelley, the writer . . .": Holmes, *Shelley*, 730.

"My poor girl . . .": Marshall, *The Life and Letters of Mary Wollstonecraft Shelley*, vol. 2, 9.

120   "I should not live . . .": Bloom, Harold, ed. *Mary Wollstonecraft Shelley*, 15.

"My William, Clara, Allegra . . .": Marshall, *The Life and Letters of Mary Wollstonecraft Shelley*, vol. 2, 41.

"After loving him . . .": Seymour, *Mary Shelley*, 316.

120 "the *best* and least selfish man . . .": Leslie A. Marchand, ed., *Byron's Letters and Journals,* vol. 1, 11.

121 "I shall live . . .": Marshall, *The Life and Letters of Mary Wollstonecraft Shelley,* vol. 2, 21.

"the old gentleman": Seymour, *Mary Shelley,* 333.

"Lo and behold . . .": Marshall, *The Life and Letters of Mary Wollstonecraft Shelley,* vol. 2, 94.

"I was much amused . . .": Ibid., 95

123 "the intimate friend . . .": Ibid., 66.

"Yet, is it true . . .": M. W. Shelley, *Mary Shelley: The Dover Reader,* 494.

124 "light footfalls . . .": M. W. Shelley, ed., *Posthumous Poems of Percy Bysshe Shelley,* 113.

". . . if a thing divine . . .": Ibid., 196.

125 "Swift as a spirit . . .": Ibid., 73.

"No man was ever more devoted than he . . .": Ibid., iv.

"to be judged of . . .": "Shelley's Posthumous Poems," 184–85.

126 "too correct in their conduct . . .": Mrs. Herbert Martin, *Memories of Seventy Years,* 81.

127 "made welcome Mrs. Shelley . . .": Charles Cowden Clarke and Mary Cowden Clarke, *Recollections of Writers,* 37–38.

128 "Be it ever so humble . . .": John Howard Payne, "Home, Sweet Home."

129 "You are perpetually in my presence . . .": Seymour, *Mary Shelley,* 370.

"Your imagination creates the admired . . .": Ibid.

130 "Be kind to me . . .": Ibid., 344.

"The great affection . . .": Bennett, ed., *The Letters of Mary Wollstonecraft Shelley,* vol. 1, 380.

"Ye Gods . . .": Ibid., 425.

131 "my loved Shelley . . .": Marshall, *The Life and Letters of Mary Wollstonecraft Shelley,* vol. 2, 114.

131 "Why am I doomed . . .": Blumberg, *Byron and the Shelleys*, 163.

CHΔPTER NINE
Secrets

132 "Permit a heart . . .": Mary Wollstonecraft Shelley, *The Fortunes of Perkin Warbeck*, vol. 3, 354.

"Of the crowding visitors . . .": Fiona MacCarthy, *Byron: Life and Legend*, 535.

134 "upon the world's love . . .": Bennett, ed., *The Letters of Mary Wollstonecraft Shelley*, vol. 1, 453.

"supremely handsome . . .": M. W. Shelley, *The Last Man*, vol. 1, 37.

135 "stony eyes . . .": Ibid., vol. 2, 20.

"He was lifted . . .": Ibid., 40.

136 "after long endurance . . .": Ibid., 199.

"The whole appears to us . . .": Untitled review of *The Last Man*, in the *Monthly Review*, January–April 1826, 335.

"monstrous fable . . .": Untitled review of *The Last Man*, in the *Literary Gazette and Journal of the Belles Lettres, Arts, Sciences, Etc.*, February 18, 1826, 102–3.

137 "more queer stingy . . .": Joan Rees, *Shelley's Jane Williams*, 128.

"Where I see suffering . . .": M. W. Shelley, *The Fortunes of Perkin Warbeck*, vol. 3, 352.

138 "The country about here . . .": Marshall, *The Life and Letters of Mary Wollstonecraft Shelley*, vol. 2, 119.

139 "My friend has proved false . . .": Ibid., 166–67.

140 "You gave ear . . .": Thomas James Wise.

141 "the most terrible . . .": Thomas Babington Macaulay, *The History of England from the Accession of James II*, vol. 4, 575.

142 "It was rather droll . . .": Bennett, ed., *The Letters of Mary Wollstonecraft Shelley*, vol. 2, 46.

143 "old Aunt": H. Buxton Forman, ed., *Letters of Edward John Trelawny*, 116.

144 "a monster to look at . . .": Gittings and Manton, *Claire Clairmont and the Shelleys*, 129.

"I always wished . . .": H. Buxton Forman, ed., *Letters of Edward John Trelawny*, 117.

"There is nothing . . .": Marshall, *The Life and Letters of Mary Wollstonecraft Shelley*, vol. 2, 193.

145 "I became aware . . .": M. W. Shelley, *The Fortunes of Perkin Warbeck*, vol. 1, iii.

146 "I feel my many weaknesses . . .": Ibid., vol. 3, 352–53.

"full of strange incident . . .": Untitled review of *The Fortunes of Perkin Warbeck*, in the *London Literary Gazette and Journal of the Belles Lettres, Arts, Sciences, Etc.*, May 22, 1830, 335.

"it may impart useful instruction . . .": *The Crayon Miscellany*, unnumbered page.

"And now, once again . . .": M. W. Shelley, *Frankenstein*, 169.

CHAPTER TEN
Memory

147 "Peace! was I ever at peace . . .": Mary Wollstonecraft Shelley, *Lodore*, vol. 1, 64.

"My heart & soul . . .": Seymour, *Mary Shelley*, 427.

148 "He was a being . . .": William Godwin, Jr., *Transfusion*, xviii.

"This is a sad blow . . .": Seymour, *Mary Shelley*, 423.

149 "Lengthening years . . .": Holden, *The Wit in the Dungeon*, 242.

"with a whole life . . .": Seymour, *Mary Shelley*, 424.

"It would be giving . . .": Mary Wollstonecraft Shelley, *Mary Shelley's Literary Lives and Other Writings*, vol. 1, 174.

150 "taught to know herself . . .": M. W. Shelley, *Lodore*, vol. 1, 40–41.

"a love of truth . . .": Ibid., vol. 3, 311.

151 "Come—My only Friend . . .": Bennett, ed., *The Letters of Mary Wollstonecraft Shelley*, vol. 2, 248.

"one of the most original . . .": Untitled review of *Lodore*, in the *London Literary Gazette and Journal of the Belles Lettres, Arts, Sciences, Etc.*, March 28, 1835, 194.

"one of the best . . .": "A Decade of Novels and Nouvellettes" in *The Museum of Foreign Literature, Science, and Art*, 104.

152 "Office Keeper . . .": St. Clair, *The Godwins and the Shelleys*, 485.

"He knew himself . . .": Feldman and Scott-Kilvert, eds., *The Journals of Mary Shelley*, vol. 2, 270.

"At the depth of twelve feet . . .": Ibid.

153 "What is there . . .": William Godwin, *Essays*, 283.

"It has been the main object . . .": Ibid., v.

154 "a garden rose . . .": M. W. Shelley, *Falkner*, 22.

"a sort of rapturous, thrilling adoration" and "a half remorse . . .": Ibid., 46.

"torn by throes . . .": Ibid., 26.

155 "Energy and highly wrought passion . . .": Untitled review of *Falkner*, in the *Literary Gazette and Journal of the Belles Lettres*, February 4, 1837, 66.

157 "most sacred duty . . .": M. W. Shelley, ed., *The Poetical Works of Percy Bysshe Shelley*, vol. 1, xvi.

"Mountain and lake . . .": Ibid., 103.

"a soul and a voice . . .": Ibid., vol. 2, 136.

"This minute and active sympathy . . .": Ibid., vol. 1, 377.

"His poems may be divided . . .": Ibid., vol. 1, x.

158 "Does Mrs. Shelley believe . . .": "Our Library Table," *Athenaeum*, April 27, 1839, 313.

"a falsification of Shelley's nature . . .": Untitled review of *The Poetical Works of Percy Bysshe Shelley*, in the *Examiner*, February 3, 1839, 70.

159 "How very much he must enjoy . . .": Bennett, ed., *The Letters of Mary Wollstonecraft Shelley*, vol. 2, 310.

"I am torn to pieces . . .": Ibid., 559.

"time may flow on . . .": Seymour, *Mary Shelley*, 471.

"the tenets and beliefs . . .": Stewart M. Hoover and Nadia Kaneva, eds., *Fundamentalisms and the Media*, 41.

160 "My heart was elevated . . .": Mary Wollstonecraft Shelley, *Rambles in Germany and Italy*, 93.

"by myriads of loving spirits . . .": Ibid., 94.

"strange and indescribable emotions . . .": Ibid., 60–61.

162 "affection and devotion . . .": Gittings and Manton, *Claire Clairmont and the Shelleys*, 178.

CHAPTER ELEVEN

Happiness

163 "The turf will soon be green . . .": M. W. Shelley, *Mathilda*, 219–20.

164 "to have wasted . . .": Seymour, *Mary Shelley*, 507.

166 "always cheerful . . .": Bennett, ed., *The Letters of Mary Wollstonecraft Shelley*, vol. 3, 158.

"Who are you . . .": Dorothy Hoobler and Thomas Hoobler, *The Monsters*, 315.

"I am Mary Shelley": Ibid.

167 "had the most beautiful deep-set eyes . . .": Ibid.

"She is in herself . . .": Rees, *Shelley's Jane Williams*, 167.

"It is old fashioned . . .": R. Glynn Grylls, *Mary Shelley: A Biography*, 251.

169 "I walk very well . . .": Charlotte Gordon, *Romantic Outlaws*, 535.

"did not do her the least good": Jones, ed., *The Letters of Mary W. Shelley*, vol. 2, 357.

170 "There is no danger now": Seymour, *Mary Shelley*, 538.

"her sweet gentle spirit . . .": Rees, *Shelley's Jane Williams*, 170.

"Disease of the brain . . .": Emily W. Sunstein, *Mary Shelley*, 384.

"It would have broken . . .": Gordon, *Romantic Outlaws*, 542.

171 "a slender and pallid . . .": William Michael Rossetti, *Some Reminiscences of William Michael Rossetti*, vol. 2, 353.

Epilogue

173 "O listen . . .": M. W. Shelley, *Mary Shelley's* Literary Lives *and Other Writings*, vol. 4, 148.

"the daughter of Godwin . . .": "Death of Mrs. Shelley," *Eclectic Magazine*, January–April 1851, 569.

177 "the dull yellow eye . . .": M. W. Shelley, *Frankenstein*, 35.

Bibliography

Angeli, Helen Rossetti. *Shelley and His Friends in Italy.* New York: Haskell House, 1973.

La Belle Assemblée. March 1818. Available online: www.rc.umd.edu/reference/chronologies/mschronology/reviews/barev.html.

Bennett, Betty T., ed. *The Letters of Mary Wollstonecraft Shelley.* 3 vols. Baltimore: Johns Hopkins University Press, 1980–88.

Bloom, Harold, ed. *Mary Wollstonecraft Shelley.* New York: Bloom's Literary Criticism, 2008.

Blumberg, Jane. *Byron and the Shelleys: The Story of a Friendship.* London: Collins and Brown, 1992.

The Bodleian Shelley Manuscripts. 23 vols. New York: Garland Publishing, 1986–2002.

Brett-Smith, H. F. B., ed. *Peacock's Memoirs of Shelley.* London: Henry Frowde, 1909.

Byron, George Gordon. *The Complete Works of Lord Byron.* Paris: Baudry's European Library, 1835.

Coleridge, Samuel Taylor. *The Rime of the Ancient Mariner.* Boston: Educational Publishing Company, 1906.

Cowden Clarke, Charles, and Mary Cowden Clarke. *Recollections of Writers.* New York: Charles Scribner's Sons, 1878.

The Crayon Miscellany. No. 2. Philadelphia: Carey, Lea, and Blanchard, 1835.

Davis, Matthew L. *The Private Journal of Aaron Burr.* 2 vols. New York: Harper and Brothers, 1838.

"A Decade of Novels and Nouvellettes." *The Museum of Foreign Literature, Science, and Art*. July–December 1835, pp. 91–106.

Dowden, Edward. *The Life of Percy Bysshe Shelley*. 2 vols. London: Kegan Paul, Trench and Co., 1886.

Elze, Karl. *Lord Byron: A Biography*. London: John Murray, 1872.

Feldman, Paula R., and Diana Scott-Kilvert, eds. *The Journals of Mary Shelley, 1814–1844*. Oxford, U.K.: Clarendon Press, 1987.

Forman, Harry Buxton, ed. *Letters of Edward John Trelawny*. London: Henry Frowde, 1910.

———, ed. *The Poetical Works of Percy Bysshe Shelley*. 4 vols. London: Reeves and Turner, 1882.

Garnett, Richard, ed. *Thomas Love Peacock: Letters to Edward Hookham and Percy B. Shelley*. Boston: Bibliophile Society, 1910.

Gittings, Robert, and Jo Manton. *Claire Clairmont and the Shelleys, 1798–1879*. Oxford, U.K.: Oxford University Press, 1992.

Godwin, William. *Essays*. London: Henry S. King and Co., 1873.

———. *An Enquiry Concerning Political Justice*. Dublin: Luke White, 1793.

Godwin, William, Jr. *Transfusion*. London: John Macrone, 1835.

Gordon, Charlotte. *Romantic Outlaws: The Extraordinary Lives of Mary Wollstonecraft & Mary Shelley*. New York: Random House, 2015.

Grylls, R. Glynn. *Mary Shelley: A Biography*. New York: Haskell House, 1969.

The Hamilton Palace Libraries: Catalogue of the Third Portion of the Beckford Library. London: Dryden Press, 1882.

Harington, C. R., ed. *The Year Without a Summer? World Climate in 1816*. Ottawa: Canadian Museum of Nature, 1992.

Hogg, Thomas Jefferson. *The Life of Percy Bysshe Shelley*. London: Edward Moxon, 1858.

Holden, Anthony. *The Wit in the Dungeon*. New York: Little, Brown and Co., 2005.

Holmes, Richard. *Shelley: The Pursuit*. New York: E. P. Dutton and Co., 1975.

Hoobler, Dorothy, and Thomas Hoobler. *The Monsters: Mary Shelley and the Curse of Frankenstein*. New York: Little, Brown and Co., 2006.

Hoover, Stewart M., and Nadia Kaneva, eds. *Fundamentalisms and the Media*. London: Continuum, 2009.

Hunt, Thornton, ed. *The Correspondence of Leigh Hunt*. 2 vols. London: Smith, Elder and Co., 1862.

Hutchinson, Thomas, ed. *Shelley: Poetical Works*. London: Oxford University Press, 1970.

Ingpen, Roger, ed. *The Letters of Percy Bysshe Shelley*. 2 vols. London: G. Bell and Sons, 1915.

Jones, Frederick L., ed. *The Letters of Mary W. Shelley*. 2 vols. Norman, OK: University of Oklahoma Press, 1944.

———, ed. *The Letters of Percy Bysshe Shelley*. 2 vols. Oxford, U.K.: Clarendon Press, 1964.

———, ed. *Maria Gisborne and Edward E. Williams, Shelley's Friends: Their Letters and Journals*. Norman, OK: University of Oklahoma Press, 1951.

Kegan Paul, C. *William Godwin: His Friends and Contemporaries*. 2 vols. London: Henry S. King and Co., 1876.

Lamb, Charles. *The Adventures of Ulysses*. London: Juvenile Library, 1819.

Lansdown, Richard, ed. *Byron's Letters and Journals: A New Selection*. Oxford, U.K.: Oxford University Press, 2015.

Lawrence, William. *Lectures on Physiology, Zoology, and the Natural History of Man*. London: Benbow, 1822.

Macaulay, Thomas Babington. *The History of England from the Accession of James II*. Vol. 4. Philadelphia: Porter and Coates, 1887.

MacCarthy, Fiona. *Byron: Life and Legend*. New York: Farrar, Straus and Giroux, 2002.

Marchand, Leslie A., ed. *Byron's Letters and Journals*. Vol. 1. Cambridge, MA: Belknap Press, 1974.

Marshall, Mrs. Julian. *The Life and Letters of Mary Wollstonecraft Shelley*. 2 vols. New York: Haskell House, 1970.

Martin, Mrs. Herbert. *Memories of Seventy Years*. New York: Griffith and Farran, 1883.

Medwin, Thomas. *The Life of Percy Bysshe Shelley*. 2 vols. London: Thomas Cautley Newby, 1847.

———. *Memoir of Percy Bysshe Shelley*. London: Whittaker, Treacher and Co., 1833.

Millingen, Julius. *Memoirs of the Affairs of Greece*. London: John Rodwell, 1831.

Moore, Thomas, ed. *Letters and Journals of Lord Byron*. 2 vols. London: John Murray, 1833.

Murray, John, ed. *Lord Byron's Correspondence*. Vol. 2. Cambridge, U.K.: Cambridge University Press, 2011.

Payne, John Howard. "Home, Sweet Home." Boston: Lee and Shepard, 1881.

"The Prince on St. Patrick's Day." *Examiner*, March 22, 1812, pp. 177–80.

Prothero, Rowland E., ed. *The Works of Lord Byron*. 13 vols. London: John Murray, 1898–1905.

Quarterly Review. Vol. 18: *October 1817–May 1818*. London: John Murray, 1818.

Reed, Henry, ed. *The Complete Poetical Works of William Wordsworth*. Philadelphia: Troutman and Hayes, 1851.

Rees, Joan. *Shelley's Jane Williams*. London: William Kimber, 1985.

"Remarks on *Frankenstein, or the Modern Prometheus; a Novel*." *Blackwood's Edinburgh Magazine*, March 1818, pp. 613–20.

Robinson, Charles E., ed. *Mary Shelley: Collected Tales and Stories*. Baltimore: Johns Hopkins University Press, 1976.

Rossetti, William Michael, ed. *The Diary of Dr. John William Polidori*. London: Elkin Mathews, 1911.

———. "Shelley's Life and Writings." *Dublin University Magazine*, February 1878, pp. 138–55.

———. *Some Reminiscences of William Michael Rossetti*. Vol. 2, London: Brown Langham and Co., 1906.

St. Clair, William. *The Godwins and the Shelleys*. New York: W. W. Norton and Co., 1989.

Scolfield, William [William Godwin]. *Bible Stories: Memorable Acts of the Ancient Patriarchs, Judges and Kings*. Wilmington, DE: Matthew R. Lockerman, 1812.

Seymour, Miranda. *Mary Shelley*. New York: Grove Press, 2000.

Shelley, Mary Wollstonecraft, ed. *Essays, Letters from Abroad, Translations and Fragments*, London: Edward Moxon, 1845.

———. *Falkner*. Doylestown, PA: Wildside, n.d.

———. *The Fortunes of Perkin Warbeck*. 3 vols. London: Henry Colburn and Richard Bentley, 1830.

———. *Frankenstein*. New York: W. W. Norton and Co., 2012.

———. *History of a Six Weeks' Tour through a Part of France, Switzerland, Germany, and Holland*. London: T. Hookham, Jr., 1817 (with Percy Bysshe Shelley).

———. *The Last Man*. 2 vols. Philadelphia: Carey, Lea and Blanchard, 1833.

———. *Lodore*. 3 vols. London: Richard Bentley, 1835.

———. *Mary Shelley: The Dover Reader*. Mineola, NY: Dover Publications, 2015.

———. *Mary Shelley's* Literary Lives *and Other Writings*. 4 vols. London: Pickering and Chatto, 2002.

———. *Mathilda*. Sydney, Australia: Accessible Publishing Systems, 2008.

———. *Maurice, or the Fisher's Cot*. Chicago: University of Chicago Press, 1998.

———, ed. *The Poetical Works of Percy Bysshe Shelley*. 4 vols. London: Edward Moxon, 1839.

———, ed. *Posthumous Poems of Percy Bysshe Shelley*. London: John and Henry L. Hunt, 1824.

———. *Rambles in Germany and Italy, in 1840, 1842, and 1843*. London: Edward Moxon, 1844.

———. "Stanzas." *The Keepsake for MDCCCXXXIX*. London: Longman, Orme, Brown, Green, and Longmans, 1839.

———. *Valperga: or, the Life and Adventures of Castruccio, Prince of Lucca*. 3 vols. London: G. and W. B. Whittaker, 1823.

Shelley, Percy Bysshe. *The Complete Poetical Works of Percy Bysshe Shelley*. 3 vols. London: John Slark, 1885.

———. "On 'Frankenstein.'" *Athenaeum*, March 10, 1832, p. 730.

"Shelley's Posthumous Poems." *Knight's Quarterly Magazine*, August–November 1824, pp. 182–88.

Stocking, Marion Kingston, ed. *The Clairmont Correspondence*. 2 vols. Baltimore: Johns Hopkins University Press, 1995.

———, ed. *The Journals of Claire Clairmont*. Cambridge, MA: Harvard University Press, 1968.

Sunstein, Emily W. *Mary Shelley: Romance and Reality*. Boston: Little, Brown and Co., 1989.

Tomalin, Claire. *Shelley and His World*. New York: Charles Scribner's Sons, 1980.

Trelawny, E. J. "Shelley's Last Days." *Athenaeum*, August 3, 1878, p. 144.

Van Doren, Mark, ed. *Correspondence of Aaron Burr and His Daughter Theodosia*. New York: Stratford Press, 1929.

Wardle, Ralph M., ed. *Godwin & Mary: Letters of William Godwin and Mary Wollstonecraft*. Lincoln, NE: University of Nebraska Press, 1966.

Wilson, Frances, ed. *Byromania: Portraits of the Artist in Nineteenth- and Twentieth-Century Culture*. Houndmills, Basingstoke, Hampshire, U.K.: Palgrave, 2000.

Wise, Thomas James, coll. *A Shelley Library*. New York: Haskell House, 1971.

Wollstonecraft, Mary. *Letters Written during a Short Residence in Sweden, Norway, and Denmark*. London: J. Johnson, 1802.

———. *Maria: The Wrongs of Woman*. Irving, TX: Sparklesoup Studios, 2004.

———. *A Vindication of the Rights of Woman*. London: Walter Scott, 1891.

The Works of Mary Wollstonecraft Shelley

Novels

Frankenstein; or, the Modern Prometheus. London: Lackington, Hughes, Harding, Mavor, and Jones, 1818.

Valperga; or, the Life and Adventures of Castruccio, Prince of Lucca. London: G. and W. B. Whittaker, 1823.

The Last Man. London: Henry Colburn, 1826.

The Fortunes of Perkin Warbeck, a Romance. London: Henry Colburn and Richard Bentley, 1830.

Lodore. London: Richard Bentley, 1835.

Falkner. London: Saunders and Otley, 1837.

Mathilda. Chapel Hill: University of North Carolina Press, 1959.

Travel Books

History of a Six Weeks' Tour through a Part of France, Switzerland, Germany, and Holland. London: T. Hookham, Jr., 1817 (with Percy Bysshe Shelley).

Rambles in Germany and Italy, in 1840, 1842, and 1843. London: Edward Moxon, 1844.

Children's Book

Maurice, or the Fisher's Cot. New York: Knopf, 1998.

Biographical Sketches, Short Stories, and Other Brief Works

Mary Shelley's Literary Lives *and Other Writings.* 4 volumes. London: Pickering and Chatto, 2002.

Letters and Journals

The Letters of Mary Wollstonecraft Shelley, edited by Betty T. Bennett. 3 volumes. Baltimore: Johns Hopkins University Press, 1980–1988.

The Journals of Mary Shelley, 1814–1844, edited by Paula R. Feldman and Diana Scott-Kilvert. Baltimore: Johns Hopkins University Press, 1995.

Picture Credits

Art and Picture Collection, the New York Public Library. "Man And Women, Brittany." The New York Public Library Digital Collections. 1913. digitalcollections.nypl.org/items/510d47e1-1389-a3d9-e040-e00a18064a99: 30

Author's collection: 6, 17, 19, 51, 69, 88, 91, 99, 102, 110, 126, 133, 134, 140, 145, 161

The Bodleian Libraries, The University of Oxford: 2795 f. 38, Frontispiece: 168; John Johnson Collection: London Book Trade L: 73; MS Abinger c. 56, fol. 11v: 71; c. 83, fol. 42r: 141; Shelley adds. e. 7, opp. P. 736: 105 (top); e. 18, p. 106: 113; Shelley Relics (d): 101; 4: 105 (bottom); 39: 156

Brewer-Leigh Hunt Collection, Special Collections Dept., University of Iowa Libraries: 66 (bottom)

INTERPHOTO/Alamy Stock Photo: 107

Keats–Shelley Memorial House, Rome, Italy/Bridgeman Images: 158

Alan King Engraving/Alamy Stock Photo: 7 (bottom)

Lebrecht Music and Arts Photo Library/Alamy Stock Photo: 165

Library of Congress: ii, 32, 34, 43 (bottom), 53, 58, 60, 67, 76, 151, 153

Musea Brugge © www.lukasweb.be—Art in Flanders VZW, photo Hugo Maertens: 130

Music Division, the New York Public Library. "John Howard Payne." The New York Public Library Digital Collections. digitalcollections.nypl.org/items/510d47e2-7eca-a3d9-e040-e00a18064a99: 129

National Library of Medicine: 142

National Portrait Gallery, London: x, 23, 38, 108, 117, 128, 166, 172

Index

Note: Page references in **bold** indicate photos and their captions.